Disciplines of the Spirit

A WORKBOOK ON
LIFE IN CHRIST

Disciplines of the Spirit

Maxie Dunnam

Cover design by Strange Last Name
Page design by PerfecType, Nashville, Tennessee

Dunnam, Maxie D.
    Disciplines of the Spirit : a workbook on life in Christ / Maxie Dunnam. – Franklin, Tennessee : Seedbed
Publishing, ©2021.

    pages ; cm. + 1 videodisc

        ISBN 9781628248371 (paperback)
        ISBN 9781628248579 (DVD)
        ISBN 9781628248388 (Mobi)
        ISBN 9781628248395 (ePub)
        ISBN 9781628248401 (uPDF)

        1. Spiritual life--Christianity. 2. Devotional exercises.
        3. Spiritual formation. 4. Christian life--Methodist authors. I. Title.

BV4501.3.D866   2021248/.34

SEEDBED PUBLISHING
Franklin, Tennessee
seedbed.com

CONTENTS

Week Three: Growth in Grace

Week Four: The Means of Grace

Week Five: Baptism and Holy Communion

Week Six: Prayer

Week Seven: Acting Our Way into Christlikeness

INTRODUCTION

Paul's understanding of the Christian life revolved around two basic concepts: (1) justification by grace through faith; and (2) a person in Christ. We become Christian by being justified by grace through faith. That begins the dynamic of our lives in Christ.

"In Christ," "in union with Christ," and "Christ in you" are the recurring phrases in Paul's vocabulary. Variations of that phrase occur no less than 172 times in the New Testament. His definition of a Christian is a person in Christ. "If anyone in in Christ, he is a new creation; the old has gone, the new has come" (2 Cor. 5:17).

New Testament scholar James S. Stewart titled his monumental study of Paul, *A Man in Christ*. He contended that this concept of the indwelling Christ is the key that unlocks the secrets of Paul's soul. He concluded, "Everything that religion meant for Paul is focused for us in such great words as these: 'I live, yet not I, but Christ liveth in me' (Gal. 2:20). 'There is, therefore, now no condemnation to them which are in Christ Jesus' (Rom. 8:11) 'He that is joined unto the Lord is one spirit' (1 Cor. 6:17)."[1]

We know the story of Paul's Damascus Road experience: dramatically being struck down by a blinding light and hearing the voice of Christ. But interestingly, we don't hear that story from Paul. Luke describes that experience in The Acts of the Apostles. Paul talks, rather, about the meaning of that experience and almost sings about it in exulting joy: "I have been crucified with Christ and I no longer live, but Christ lives in me. The life I now live in the body, I live by faith in the Son of God, who loved me and gave himself for me" (Gal. 2:20 NIV).

This core theme of Paul—life in Christ—is the subject of this workbook. I have used my workbook style to explore the issue. The very title, *Disciplines of the Spirit: A Workbook on Life in Christ*, suggests that it may require more than expressing and elaborating on ideas. Special attention is given to particular disciplines Christians call means of grace, because they are especially experienced as channels through which God's grace is conveyed to us.

They are disciplines of the Spirit, as Wesley described them: "outward signs, words and actions ordained by God, and appointed to the end to be ordinary channels whereby he might convey to man preventing, justifying or sanctifying grace."[2]

I urge you to stay aware that the workbook format is important to appropriating meaning of the content, and our growth in our lives in Christ. It is designed for individual and group use. Let's look at the process. It is simple but important.

I have learned from my long years of teaching and ministry with small groups that a six- to eight-week period for a group study is the most manageable and effective. Also, people can best appropriate content and truth in small doses. That is the reason for organizing the material in segments to be read daily.

The plan for using the workbook calls for a seven-week commitment. You are asked to give at least thirty to forty-five minutes each day to reflect on some dimension of spiritual disciplines and the means of grace. For most persons, engagement with the workbook will probably come at the beginning of the day. However, if it is not possible for you to give the time at the beginning of the day, do it whenever the time is available, but do it regularly.

This is not only an intellectual pursuit; it is also a spiritual journey, the purpose of which is to incorporate the content into your daily life. This journey is personal, but my hope is that you will share it with some fellow pilgrims who will meet together once each week during the seven weeks of the study. The workbook is arranged into seven major divisions, each designed to guide you for one week. These divisions contain seven sections, one for each day of the week. Each day of the week will have three major aspects: (1) reading, (2) reflecting and recording ideas and thoughts about the material and your own understanding and experience, (3) some practical suggestions for incorporating ideas from the reading material into your daily life.

The content for each day will not be too much to read, but it will be enough to challenge thought and action. The degree of meaning you receive from this workbook depends largely on your faithfulness in reflecting and recording. On some days there may be more suggestions than you can deal with in the time you have available. Do what is most meaningful for you, and do not feel guilty about the rest.

Always remember that this pilgrimage is personal. What you write in your workbook is your private property. You may not wish to share it with anyone. For this reason, no two people should attempt to share the same workbook. The importance of what you write is not what it may mean to someone else but what it means to you. Writing, even if only brief notes or single-word reminders, helps us clarify our feelings and thinking.

The significance of the reflecting-and-recording dimension will grow as you move along. Even beyond the seven weeks, you will find meaning in looking back to what you wrote on a particular day in response to a particular situation.

Sharing with Others

There is a sense in which this workbook can be a spiritual guide, for you can use it as a private venture without participating in a group. The value of the workbook will be enhanced, however, if you share the adventure with eight to twelve others. In this way, you will profit from the growing insights of others, and they will profit from yours.

The text includes a guide for group sharing at the end of each week. If this is a group venture, everyone should begin their personal involvement with the book on the same day, so that when you come together to share as a group, all will have been dealing with the same material and will be at the same place in the text. It will be helpful to have an initial get-acquainted group meeting to begin the adventure.

Group sessions for this workbook are designed to last ninety minutes (with the exception of the initial meeting). Those sharing in the group should covenant to attend all sessions unless an emergency prevents attendance. There will be seven weekly sessions in addition to this first get-acquainted time.

Group Leader's Tasks

One person may provide the leadership for the entire seven weeks, or leaders may be assigned from week to week. The leader's tasks are:

1. Read the directions and determine ahead of time how to handle the session. It may not be possible to use all the suggestions for sharing and praying together. Feel free to select those you think will be most meaningful and those for which you have adequate time.

2. Model a style of openness, honesty, and warmth. A leader does not ask anyone to share what he or she is not willing to share. Usually, as leader, be the first to share, especially as it relates to personal experiences.

3. Moderate the discussion.

4. Encourage reluctant members to participate and try to prevent a few group members from doing all the talking.

5. Keep the sharing centered in personal experience rather than academic debate.

6. Honor the time schedule. If it appears necessary to go longer than ninety minutes, the leader should get consensus for continuing another twenty or thirty minutes.

7. See that the meeting time and place are known by all, especially if meetings are held in different homes.

8. Make sure that the necessary materials for meetings are available and that the meeting room is arranged ahead of time.

It is a good idea to hold weekly meetings in the homes of the participants. (Hosts or hostesses may make sure there are as few interruptions as possible from children, telephones, pets, and so forth.) If the meetings are held in a church, plan to be in an informal setting. Participants are asked to dress casually, to be comfortable and relaxed. If refreshments are planned, serve them after the formal meeting. In this way, those who wish to stay longer for informal discussion may do so, while those who need to keep to the time schedule will be free to leave, having had the full value of the meeting time.

Suggestions for Initial Get-Acquainted Meeting

Since the initial meeting is for the purpose of getting acquainted and beginning the shared pilgrimage, here is a way to get started. (If name tags are needed, provide them.)

1. Have each person in the group give his or her full name and the name by which each wishes to be called. Do away with titles. Address all persons by their first name or nickname. (Each person should make a list of the names somewhere in his/her workbook.)

2. Let each person in the group share one of the happiest, most exciting, or most meaningful experiences he/she has had during the past three or four weeks. After all persons have shared in this way, let the entire group sing the doxology ("Praise God, from Whom All Blessings Flow") or a chorus of praise.

3. After this experience of happy sharing, ask each person who will to share his/her expectations of this workbook study. Why did he or she become a part of it? What does each expect to gain from it? What are the reservations?

4. The leader should now review the introduction to the workbook and ask if there are questions about directions and procedures (this means that the leader should have read the introduction prior to the meeting). If persons have not received copies of the workbook, the books should be handed out now. Remember that every person must have his/her own workbook.

5. Day One in the workbook is the day following this initial meeting, and the next meeting should be held on Day Seven of the First Week. If the group must choose another weekly meeting time other than seven days from this initial session, the reading assignment should be brought in harmony with that so that the weekly meetings are always on Day Seven, and Day One is always the day following a weekly meeting.

6. Nothing binds a group together more than praying for one another. The leader should encourage each participant to write the names of each person in the group in his/her workbook and commit to praying for them by name daily during these seven weeks.

After checking to see that everyone knows the time and place of the next meeting, the leader may close with prayer, thanking God for each person in the group, for the opportunity for growth, and for the possibility of growing in our lives in Christ.

Disciplines of the Spirit

Week One
Going on to Salvation

Salvation Is More Than a One-Time Event

Then we will no longer be infants, tossed back and forth by the waves, and blown here and there by every wind of teaching and by the cunning and craftiness of people in their deceitful scheming. Instead, speaking the truth in love, we will grow to become in every respect the mature body of him who is the head, that is, Christ. From him the whole body, joined and held together by every supporting ligament, grows and builds itself up in love, as each part does its work.

—Eph. 4:14–16

This study's primary focus is on the spiritual disciplines and the means of grace, the purposes of which are spiritual growth. So we begin with looking at the nature of salvation. Too many see salvation as a one-time event—that moment we acknowledge ourselves as sinners, confess our sin, repent, and accept Christ as our Savior. That, however, is the beginning experience; we do not suddenly emerge as full-grown Christians. We call experiencing spiritual maturity in its fullness "going on to salvation."

John Wesley had a clear picture of what he called the "way of salvation." Though he seldom used the word *conversion*, he placed a strong emphasis on justification. Many Christian thinkers do not do so, but Wesley distinguished regeneration and the new birth from justification. He began his sermon "The New Birth":

If any doctrines within the whole compass of Christianity may be properly termed fundamental, they are doubtless these two—the doctrine of justification, and that of the new birth: the former relating to that great work which God does *for* us, in forgiving our sins; the latter, to the great work which God does *in* us, in renewing our fallen nature.[1]

Though distinctive, the doctrines of justification and new birth belong together. God acts for us to forgive us, and at the same time begins the restoration of the divine image within us. This is the reason the new birth is such a powerful image. As our physical birth is the momentous beginning of our physical life on earth, our new life in Christ is the beginning of our soul's life for spiritual growth. We are, by God's grace, redeemed from sin and justified in relation to him; we are born of the Spirit.

Wesley defined the nature of the new birth in this fashion:

It is that great change which God works in the soul when he brings it into life; when he raises it from the death of sin to the life of righteousness. It is the change wrought in the whole soul by the almighty Spirit of God when it is "created anew in Christ Jesus"; when it is "renewed after the image of God, in righteousness and true holiness"; when the love of the world is changed into the love of God; pride into humility; passion into meekness; hatred, envy, malice, into a sincere, tender, disinterested love for all mankind.[2]

Even here, in the description of these elements of salvation—justification and new birth—there is the dynamic of growth, *going on to salvation*. We may be justified by grace through faith (see Romans 3:24; Ephesians 2:8) and be converted to Christ in the miracle of a moment, but the making of a saint, Christian maturity, is the task of a lifetime. That's the reason spiritual disciplines and the means of grace are essential. As Jesus talked about being "born again" (John 3:3), Paul, in his epistle to the Ephesians, calls us to no longer be infants, but to "grow up . . . into Christ" (Eph. 4:15 RSV).

Reflecting and Recording

Spend some time reflecting on your spiritual journey. Can you recall a time when you definitely claimed the Christian faith and named yourself a Christian? Write a few notes about that experience, perhaps some dates, feelings, occasions, and persons who may have been involved.

During the Day

Choose someone with whom you are comfortable sharing, tell them about this study you are beginning, and discuss what you have thought and recorded about your spiritual journey.

Salvation Began at the Beginning

"No one can come to me unless the Father who sent me draws them, and I will raise them up at the last day. It is written in the Prophets: 'They will all be taught by God.' Everyone who has heard the Father and learned from him comes to me."

—John 6:44–45

Salvation began at the beginning. The Nicene Creed, the creed most used by Christians, states this as it talks about God coming to us in Jesus Christ:

For us and for our salvation
he came down from heaven;
he became incarnate by the Holy Spirit and the virgin Mary,
and was made human.

God the Father almighty, maker of heaven and earth, loves us so much that he comes to us in Jesus Christ. We are saved by his grace. This grace is incomprehensible; in fact, theologian Karl Barth pointedly remarked in his book *The Epistle to the Romans*: "Only when grace is recognized as incomprehensible is it grace."[3] Even so, we experience grace expressed in different ways, and we have different ways of talking about it.

In his sermon "The Scripture Way of Salvation," John Wesley summarized the goal of genuine Christian religion: "The end is, in one word, salvation." In its broadest sense, Wesley understood salvation as the entire redeeming work of God in a human life, "from the first dawning of grace in the soul, till it is consummated in glory." He includes within his concept of salvation "all the drawings of the Father"—which he terms "preventing grace"—in the heart of a person as yet uncommitted to God.[4]

God's grace works in us even before justifying grace and the new birth. We call this *prevenient grace,* a term describing God's first attempts to reach us, call us, and save us. Jesus said, "No one can come to me unless the Father who sent me draws them, and I will raise them up at the last day" (John 6:44). God always makes the first move toward us.

Grace is undeserved love; the unmerited favor God bestows. The word *prevenient* is a combination of two Latin root words: *prae,* meaning "before," and *venire,* "to come." Prevenient means that which comes first or in advance. So, prevenient grace is that first move God makes in our direction.

Prevenient grace may be that first slight twinge of conscience, or the vague discontent or growing questioning about our lifestyle, or concern about our relationship with God. Grace is God calling our name.

Later, we will discuss Scripture as one of the primary means of grace. One of the ways I make this means effective in my life is to read the Bible in different translations. Consider the following passage, which is an illuminating expression of prevenient grace:

For I am not ashamed of the Gospel. I see it as the very power of God working for the salvation of everyone who believes it, both Jew and Greek. I see in it God's plan for imparting righteousness to men, a process begun and continued by their faith. For, as the scripture says: "The just shall live by faith." (Rom. 1:16–17 PHILLIPS)

Many translations of Romans 1:16 have Paul stating simply that the gospel is "the power of God *for* salvation." Note how Phillips translates it, "the power of God *working for* the salvation of everyone who believes." C. K. Barrett, an outstanding British New Testament scholar, has what I believe is a more meaningful translation: "For I am not ashamed of the Gospel, since it is the operation of God's power *working towards salvation*, effective for everyone who has faith—Jews first, and then the Gentiles too."[5]

This is a powerful expression of prevenient grace: "*God's* power *working towards* salvation, effective for everyone who has faith." Even before God's grace works for our justification and new birth, his grace is working to bring us to that point where we acknowledge our sin and begin to realize we *need* to be saved from our sin.

Note in the Phillips and Barrett translations that salvation is presented as a *process*—not a dynamic of fixed steps, but that of one thing happening before another can work. What is important to recognize is that God is taking the initiative, always offering his loving power for our full salvation.

The gospel itself is the "operation of God's power working *towards* salvation," as Barrett translates Paul. This is not merely an announcement, or a proclamation, that salvation will come at some time in the future. God's power is at work *now*; God is taking the initiative. This working of God is not dependent upon any human activity or condition; it is not because we have chosen, but because God wills and longs for our salvation.

God acted once and for all to provide a means for our salvation, offering his Son Jesus as his sacrificial gift of love. Through the Holy Spirit, he acts in an ongoing way to bring us to the point where we will accept his gift.

Reflecting and Recording

Yesterday you were asked to reflect on your Christian journey as you came into the Christian faith. In that reflection, were there occasions, situations, or persons that you would now consider dynamics of what we are calling prevenient *grace* (God going before you, bringing you to a point of decision and commitment)? Make a note of those things.

During the Day

If you thought of persons who played a role in your coming into the Christian faith, find a way to tell them thank you today.

Make a decision that throughout the day (perhaps while waiting at a traffic light or for an appointment, or when saying a blessing over a meal), you will bring this thought to mind: the gospel itself is the "operation of God's power working *towards* [my] salvation."

Assurance

Therefore, brothers and sisters, we have an obligation—but it is not to the flesh, to live according to it. For if you live according to the flesh, you will die; but if by the Spirit you put to death the misdeeds of the body, you will live.

For those who are led by the Spirit of God are the children of God. The Spirit you received does not make you slaves, so that you live in fear again; rather, the Spirit you received brought about your adoption to sonship. And by him we cry, "Abba, Father." The Spirit himself testifies with our spirit that we are God's children. Now if we are children, then we are heirs—heirs of God and co-heirs with Christ, if indeed we share in his sufferings in order that we may also share in his glory.

—Rom. 8:12–17

Most people in the Methodist/Wesleyan tradition of the Christian faith know at least the broad outline of the life of our founder, John Wesley. Having been nurtured by his mother, Susanna, and his father, Samuel (a priest in the Church of England), John had a conversion to the ideal of holy living in 1725, while a student at Oxford University. There are few examples in history of a more disciplined religious person: he rose at 4:00 a.m., read the New Testament in Greek for an hour, and then prayed for an hour with his brother Charles and others who had joined him in what was derisively called the Holy Club. He spent time visiting prisons and gave to the poor all of his money except that which was absolutely necessary for his own living. He was almost neurotically preoccupied with the right use of his time.

John Wesley was a man desperately seeking both salvation and assurance of his salvation. He was tirelessly bent upon achieving that, and drove himself as a merciless taskmaster in all the spiritual disciplines and services that could be imagined. He even went to the American colonies as a missionary to Indigenous Peoples. Having failed in that endeavor, John returned home from Georgia, downcast in mind, despondent in spirit, pierced to his heart with the futility of all his efforts and the emptiness of his soul.

It was in that despondent mood that he went to a prayer meeting on Aldersgate Street, London, on May 24, 1738. A layperson read Martin Luther's preface to the epistle to the Romans, and Wesley described later what happened in his own life: "I felt my heart strangely warmed. I felt I did trust in Christ, Christ alone for my salvation; and an assurance was given me that he had taken away *my* sins, even *mine*, and saved *me* from the law of sin and death."[6]

Salvation is at the center of Methodist theology, and Wesley's understanding is often discussed with four claims: (1) all people need to be saved from sin, (2) all people may be saved from sin, (3) all people may know they are saved from sin, and (4) all people may be saved to the uttermost.[7]

Aldersgate was the watershed experience that gave Wesley assurance of his salvation. No wonder this became one of the "Four Alls" of Wesley's understanding of salvation: all can *know they are saved.*

The apostle Paul might say that Wesley "did not receive the spirit of slavery to fall back into fear, but . . . the spirit of sonship"—the sonship that would enable him to "cry, 'Abba! Father!'" (Rom. 8:15 RSV).

Reflecting and Recording

Assurance is the privilege of all Christians, though not all Christians claim it. Spend a few minutes reflecting on whether you are claiming that gift.

The witness of assurance is continually verified in different ways. Consider these ways and put a check by those present in your life:

____ 1. I know that I have repented of my sins, and will continue to repent daily.

____ 2. I am aware of change in my life, and the awareness of assurance grows within me as I see changes continually happening.

____ 3. I am aware of a new character being produced in me, as the fruits of the Spirit are growing in my life.

____ 4. I find joy in the service of God.

During the Day

If you did not check all of the verifications of assurance listed, what can you do now and as you move through the day to act on them?

Work Out in Fact What Is True in Principle

Don't you know that all of us who were baptized into Christ Jesus were baptized into his death? We were therefore buried with him through baptism into death in order that, just as Christ was raised from the dead through the glory of the Father, we too may live a new life.

—Rom. 6:3–4

The process of saint-making, Christian maturity, is to work out in fact what is already true in principle. Through justifying grace, in the position of our relationship to God in Jesus Christ, we are new persons. Now our condition, the actual life we live, must be brought into harmony with our new position.

You may have already questioned my use of the word *saint*. That word means different things to different people. In a general way, Paul called the Christians to whom he was writing in some of his New Testament letters "saints" (in Ephesus, in Philippi, in Colossae).

Paul contended that we are to become new creatures in Christ Jesus. In fact, that's the way he defined a Christian to the Romans: "just as Christ was raised from the dead through the glory of the Father, we too may live a new life." He expressed it this way to the Corinthians: "Therefore, if anyone is in Christ, the new creation has come: The old has gone, the new is here!" (2 Cor. 5:17). The aim of the Christian life is nothing less than to be new creatures in Christ Jesus. Discipline and using the means of grace are to shape us fully as new creatures in Christ Jesus. I use the word *saint* in that fashion.

Most preaching and teaching too often puts the emphasis on our coming into the Christian life—in confessing, repenting, trusting Christ as Savior, and receiving his forgiveness. The theological or biblical term for God's work in this dynamic is *justification*. When we think and talk about salvation, this is often where we center. This is limited thinking. As already stated, Wesley used the term *salvation* in a broader and deeper way, referring to the entire saving activity of God in human lives: "By salvation I mean, not barely . . . deliverance from hell, or going to heaven, but a present deliverance from sin, a restoration of the soul to its . . . original purity; a recovery of the divine nature; the renewal of our soul after the image of God, in righteousness and true holiness, in justice, mercy, and truth."[8]

Salvation is not to be understood as something coming in the future. God takes the initiative and is working now. This working of God is not dependent upon any human activity or condition; it is not because we have chosen, but because God wills and longs for our salvation. Through the Holy Spirit, he acts in an ongoing way to bring us to the point where we will accept his gift. Having the Holy Spirit continues his work, empowering us to move on to full salvation. So, we're not only talking about prevenient and justifying grace, but also *sanctifying* grace, which we will address tomorrow.

Reflecting and Recording

Spend a few minutes reflecting on Paul's claim: "just as Christ was raised from the dead through the glory of the Father, we too may live a new life" (Rom. 6:4). If you have claimed his salvation by grace through faith, thus becoming a Christian, in what way are you living a new life?

During the Day

Paul expressed the fact that Christians are new persons in Christ: "Therefore, if anyone is in Christ, the new creation has come: The old has gone, the new is here!" (2 Cor. 5:17). Keep that vision in your mind as you move through the day: *I am a new person.*

Saved to the Uttermost

Therefore let us move beyond the elementary teachings about Christ and be taken forward to maturity, not laying again the foundation of repentance from acts that lead to death, and of faith in God instruction about cleansing rites, the laying on of hands, the resurrection of the dead, and eternal judgment.

—Heb. 6:1–2

Of the Four Alls in the summary of Wesley's understanding of salvation, the third and fourth are the most distinctive: all people may know they are saved from sin, and all people may be saved to the uttermost. On Day Three, we considered assurance—the fact that we can know we are saved. Today, we consider "saved to the uttermost" (see Hebrews 7:25 KJV). For Wesley, this meant Christian perfection.

In his introductory comment to Wesley's sermon "A Plain Account of Christian Perfection," Albert Outler wrote:

If, for Wesley, salvation was the total restoration of the deformed image of God in us, and if its fullness was the recovery of our negative power not to sin and our positive power to love God supremely, this denotes that furthest reach of grace and its triumphs in this life that Wesley chose to call "Christian Perfection."⁹

Wesley particularly stressed the idea that "all can be saved to the uttermost," calling it, "going on to perfection." He emphasized the transformative work of the Holy Spirit. We can better understand the full impact of that transformation by reflecting on the distinction between God's action *for* the sinner—pardon and justification—and God's action *in* the pardoned sinner's heart—restoration of the broken image of God and of the human power to avoid and resist intentional sin. Again, Albert Outler expressed it clearly: "We have no part in our justification before God, save the passive act of accepting and trusting the merits of Christ. But we have a crucial part to play in the further business of 'growing up into Christ, into the stature of the perfect man.'"[10]

Christian perfection is another term for *sanctification*. "Just as justification and regeneration are thresholds for the Christian life in earnest ('what God does for us'), so also sanctification is 'what God does in us,' to mature and fulfill the human potential according to his primal design."[11]

As stated on Day Two, through justification and the new birth, we are new persons; now our condition, *the actual life we live*, must be brought into harmony with our new position. In the dynamic process of sanctification—Christian perfection—we practice spiritual disciplines and the means of grace to work out in fact what is true in principle.

Reflecting and Recording

Consider again C. K. Barrett's translation of Romans 1:16: "For I am not ashamed of the Gospel, since it is the operation of God's power *working towards salvation*, effective for everyone who has faith—Jews first, and then the Gentiles too."[12] Reflect on this by honestly asking: How is God's power working toward salvation in my life?

All need to be saved - original sin -

All can be saved - universal salvation

All can know they are saved - Assurance

All can be saved completely - Christian perfection

During the Day

As you continue reflecting in this fashion, find someone today with whom to discuss the notion of God working toward salvation in the context of the popular thought that salvation is a finished, one-time event.

We Grow by Discipline

Formerly, when you did not know God, you were slaves to those who by nature are not gods. But now that you know God—or rather are known by God—how is it that you are turning back to those weak and miserable forces? Do you wish to be enslaved by them all over again? You are observing special days and months and seasons and years! I fear for you, that somehow I have wasted my efforts on you. . . .

My dear children, for whom I am again in the pains of childbirth until Christ is formed in you, how I wish I could be with you now and change my tone, because I am perplexed about you!

—Gal. 4:8–11, 19–20

A little girl had been giving her mother a hard time all morning. Finally, her mother said, "Please behave yourself. Don't you know that every time you misbehave, I get another gray hair in my head?"

"My," the little girl said, "you sure must have been a bad little girl. Just look at all the gray hairs Grandmother has!"

Apart from the obvious lesson that we parents need to be careful in the way we teach our children, the story is a good introduction to one of the most profound truths of Scripture: "My little children, with whom I am again in travail until Christ be formed in you!" (Gal. 4:19 RSV).

With sharpness and clarity, Paul stated the passion of his life and his vision for a new humanity. This translation of the verse has an even more poignant feeling: "Oh, my dear children, I feel the pangs of childbirth all over again till Christ be formed within you" (PHILLIPS).

Paul's great definition of a Christian was a person "in Christ." He expressed it over and over again: "If anyone is in Christ, he is a new creation" (2 Cor. 5:17 RSV); "And the secret is simply this: Christ in you! Yes, Christ in you bringing with him the hope of all the glorious things to come" (Col. 1:27 PHILLIPS); and, "There is therefore now no condemnation for those who are in Christ Jesus" (Rom. 8:1 RSV).

We will return to these images often during the next weeks of our study: "being conformed to the image of Christ" (see Romans 8:29) and "having Christ formed in us" (see Galatians 4:19). We cultivate the presence of Christ and are formed in him by discipline, particularly through the means of grace.

Christians do not suddenly emerge mature; we grow. Our "going on to salvation" is our going on in sanctifying grace, going on to sainthood. For this journey to be effective, we must claim the reality that discipline is an absolute necessity for the Christian way. As previously stated, being converted to Christ may be the miracle of a moment, but the making of a saint is the task of a lifetime. Paul talked about that process in different ways: we are to grow up in Christ (see Ephesians 4:15); to become mature in Christ (see Colossians 1:28); and to have the mind of Christ in us (see Philippians 2:5). He used the metaphor of childbirth to express his groaning desire that Christians grow to "the measure of the stature of the fullness of Christ" (Eph. 4:13). "Oh, my dear children, I feel the pangs of childbirth all over again till Christ be formed within you" (Gal. 4:19 PHILLIPS).

It is crucial that we think rightly of discipline; it is not an end within itself. Too often within our Christian history, we have considered discipline an end rather than a means, using it as a proof of our sainthood. Albert Day, one of my mentors, spoke clearly about this misunderstanding. In *Discipline and Discovery*, a book he wrote as a manual for The Disciplined Order of Christ in 1947, he cautioned: (1) discipline must not be practiced for its own sake; (2) discipline must not be confused with repression; and (3) discipline must never be conceived as a denial or destruction of your own uniqueness.

The third warning is particularly important since the purpose of this daily workbook is to help the reader grow spiritually, with the emphasis of *growing up in Christ*. The goal

* be a servant

of our life is to be formed in Christ. That does not mean a denial or destruction of your own uniqueness, but your own being taking on the shape of Christ.

Reflecting and Recording

Spend some time examining your own patterns of discipline. Put a check by any of the following that may be descriptive:

_____ I am a very disciplined person.

_____ I am sporadic in discipline.

_____ I am disciplined in some areas.

_____ I work at it, but it is tough and I'm always struggling.

_____ I am disciplined in my efforts at Christian growth.

_____ I know that spiritual discipline is essential, but I am doing little about it.

Write a brief prayer of confession based on this self-examination.

During the Day

Look over those items that you checked. Is there anything you might do today as the beginning of a corrective response?

A Price for Everything

"The kingdom of heaven is like treasure hidden in a field. When a man found it,
he hid it again, and then in his joy went and sold all he had and bought that field.
"Again, the kingdom of heaven is like a merchant looking for fine pearls. When
he found one of great value, he went away and sold everything he had and bought it."
—Matt. 13:44–46

There is an old adage which has God saying, "Take what you wish—take it and pay for it." It's good to keep this in mind as we continue reflecting on the necessity of discipline.

There is also truth in the saying that the best things in life are free, but it isn't absolute truth. Certainly, we can't buy love, but isn't there really a price tag on love? How can we appropriate the love of a husband or a wife without paying the price of attention, tenderness, care, and the disciplined giving of our time?

How can we appropriate the beauty of God's creation? To be sure, it is an extravagant gift on the part of God. But how dull are we to that beauty? How often do we fail to allow that beauty to bathe our souls because we do not have eyes to see? We haven't taken the time to sit quietly and take in the beauty God is offering us through his creation.

Even those things that we think are free—indeed, those things which are given as gifts—require something from us if we would appropriate them. It is helpful to think of discipline in that way. The parables of the hidden treasure and the pearl of great price make the case. Jesus was underscoring the fact that to enter the kingdom is worth any sacrifice we might have to make. The man who found the treasure hidden in the field sold all that he had in order to raise the money to purchase the field. The man who found the pearl of great price sold all his other pearls, plus everything else that he had, in order to buy the prized pearl.

That's the perspective we need in considering discipline. Yes, at the core of its meaning is self-denial, but it's important to remember that we experience the freedom of joy and celebration only as we are willing to see the kingdom as a pearl of great price for which we are willing to exchange all else. Discipline enables us to exchange lesser values, habits, styles, attitudes, ways of relating, limited understandings, and closed minds for the pearl of great price: a life shaped by and in Christ.

Richard Foster was on target when he titled his now-classic book *Celebration of Discipline.* He said it well:

[We should not] think of the Spiritual Disciplines as some dull drudgery aimed at exterminating laughter from the face of the earth. Joy is the keynote of all the Disciplines. The purpose of the Disciplines is liberation from the stifling slavery to self-interest and fear. When the inner spirit is liberated from all that weighs it down, it can hardly be described as dull drudgery. Singing, dancing, even shouting characterize the Disciplines of the spiritual life.[13]

Reflecting and Recording

Have you had any experience in life that confirms the adage, "Take what you wish—take it and pay for it"?

In what area of your life (nature, love, friendship, God's presence, etc.) have you cultivated discipline in order to have the full value of a gift?

Have joy and discipline been connected in your life? If so, how?

During the Day

Do something today (write a note, make a phone call, see a person, make a gift, etc.) that you have been intending to do, but have not been disciplined enough to do it.

WEEK ONE
Group Sharing

Introduction

Personal sharing is a significant aspect of this study experience, and this guide is simply an effort to facilitate personal sharing. The leader should not be rigid in following these suggestions, but should especially seek to be sensitive to what is going on in the lives of the participants and to focus the group's sharing on those experiences. Ideas are important and we should wrestle with them, but it is important that the group meeting not become a debate about ideas. The emphasis should be on persons—experiences, feelings, and meanings.

As the group comes to the place where all can share honestly and openly what is happening in their lives, the experience will grow more meaningful. This does not mean sharing only the good or positive; also share the struggles, the difficulties, or the negatives. Discipline is not easy, and it would be deceptive to pretend it is; growth requires effort. Don't be afraid to share your questions, reservations, and dry periods, as well as that in which you find meaning.

Sharing Together

If the group did not have an introductory meeting, have each person give his or her full name and the name by which they wish to be called. Write the names in this book to use as a prayer list through this seven-week study.

1. Leader, read the section from the Nicene Creed on Day Two then invite two or three persons to share their journey of coming into the Christian faith as they reflected on Days One and Two.
2. Spend ten to fifteen minutes discussing William Fitzgerald's Four Alls of Wesley's understanding of salvation from Day Three and that assurance is the privilege of all believers.
3. Spend ten to fifteen minutes discussing being "saved to the uttermost" (sanctifying grace). Don't get involved in discussing whether you believe this or not, but focus on what it means for God to be *working toward* salvation in your life.
4. Invite as many persons as are willing to do so to share their spiritual journey, referring back to the notes they made in Reflecting and Recording on Day One: recall a time when you definitely claimed the Christian faith and named yourself a Christian.

Praying Together

Each week the group is asked to pray together. Corporate prayer is one of the great blessings of Christian community. There is power in corporate prayer, and it is important that this dimension be included in our shared pilgrimage.

It is also important that you feel comfortable in this and that no pressure be placed on anyone to pray aloud. Silent corporate prayer may be as vital and meaningful as verbal corporate prayer. God does not need our spoken words to hear our prayers. Silence, where thinking is centered and attention is focused, may provide our deepest periods of prayer.

There is power, however, in a community on a common journey who speak aloud their thoughts and feelings to God in the presence of their fellow pilgrims. Verbal prayers should be offered spontaneously as a person chooses to pray aloud. Don't practice, "Let's go around the circle now, and each one pray."

Suggestions for a time of group prayer will be given each week. The leader should regard these only as suggestions. What is happening in the meeting—the mood, the needs that are expressed, the timing—should determine the direction of the group's prayer. Here are some possibilities as you close your time together:

1. The leader (or someone who has been specifically invited by the leader) will begin the prayer time with a prayer of thanksgiving for bringing this group together, and simply pray that the group will share honestly and offer themselves in loving fellowship.

2. Think back over the sharing that has taken place during the session. What personal needs or concerns have been shared? Any participant who heard a need or concern expressed by another can speak this aloud. After each mention of a need, the leader will invite the group to silently pray for that person and concern.

3. When the focused praying is over, the group can pray the Lord's Prayer together.

Alice & Michele
Heather
Cheryl's girls
Joiner family - son died

Week Two

Walking in the Ways of God

Discipline and Discipleship

"Enter through the narrow gate. For wide is the gate and broad is the road that leads to destruction, and many enter through it. But small is the gate and narrow the road that leads to life, and only a few find it."

—Matt. 7:13–14

Last week we reflected on salvation and the notion that discipline is essential in the Christian life. We closed Day Seven noting that the purpose of discipline is to liberate us—to free us from, rather than sentence us to, bondage.

Two words are connected as we think about this dynamic: *disciples* and *discipleship.* Persons who are followers of Jesus, seeking to have their lives shaped by him, are called *disciples.* That's what Jesus' closest companions were called. The Great Commission Jesus gave his followers was to go into the world and "make disciples of all nations" (see Matthew 28:19-20).

What we do in service to Christ as we grow in being shaped by him, we call our *discipleship.* John Wesley called this "walking in the ways of God."[1] If we are serious about discipleship, we will have already discovered (or will soon discover) that we can't go it alone. Community is essential for teaching, support, and accountability.

Discipline and community are intimately related. That's the reason for this study on discipline, the means of grace, and life in Christ. Wesley expressed it: "The soul and body make a man, and the spirit and discipline make a Christian."[2]

Jesus' message about the narrow gate and wide road is clear. In life there is a broad and easy way; most of us take that way most of the time. There is a narrow, hard way; too few of us take it. Following the narrow, hard way leads to life. The difference between these two ways is that of the disciplined life and the undisciplined life.

An old adage claims that practice makes perfect. It rolls off our tongues so easily, yet if we really hear, it lays a great claim upon us. Unlike the negative way we normally think about habits, discipline and practicing the means of grace are holy habits with redemptive results.

We know, for example, the arduous practice to which a master musician must be committed. As we listen to a great pianist, we know that the superb performance did not come without the toil and sweat of repetitive labor. Someone put it this way: "You can't buy a fiddle today, and expect to give a concert in Carnegie Hall next week." What we know to be true in athletics and the arts is also true of our Christian life: we grow by disciplined effort, by decision of the will, by habits.

Reflecting and Recording

When I ask, "Who is the most disciplined person you know?" who is the first person that comes to your mind? Name that person here: _____ . Spend a few minutes thinking about what caused you to name her/him.

Name the person here who is the most *spiritually* disciplined person you know: _____ . If the two names are different, what about the two individuals is similar?

During the Day

Call one of these persons today to tell them about your journey through this study and how they came to mind.

Heart-Work

But if, in seeking to be justified in Christ, we Jews find ourselves also among the sinners, doesn't that mean that Christ promotes sin? Absolutely not! If I rebuild what I destroyed, then I really would be a lawbreaker.

For through the law I died to the law so that I might live for God. I have been crucified with Christ and I no longer live, but Christ lives in me. The life I now live in the body, I live by faith in the Son of God, who loved me and gave himself for me. I do not set aside the grace of God, for if righteousness could be gained through the law, Christ died for nothing!

—Gal. 2:17–21

Today, and for the remainder of this week, we continue reflecting on discipline and discipleship. The theme of the week is John Wesley's term: "walking in the ways of God." We will focus on particular expressions of discipline and characteristics of disciplined persons. Throughout our study we will focus on persons named as saints by Christian history to provide wisdom and guidance. Again, don't let the word confuse or divert you. I'm sure most of the Christians Paul called saints in his New Testament letters were folks like you and me.

Through our discipline and practice of the means of grace, we are opening our whole being to the Holy Spirit to reform our hearts to obedience and love. The Puritan spiritual writers labeled this "heart-work." John Flavel, a seventeenth-century English Puritan, gave this perspective: "The greatest difficulty in conversion is to win the heart to God; and the greatest difficulty after conversion is to keep the heart with God. . . ; heart-work is hard work indeed."[3]

The purpose of our heart-work is to move us on to holiness, which is full surrender of our will to Christ so that all of who we are belongs to God. Holiness requires the full surrender of our independent self-will so that God can eradicate our self-orientation. Paul was commenting autobiographically when he wrote: "I have been crucified with Christ and I no longer live, but Christ lives in me" (Gal. 2:20a). That is the testimony of saints throughout the ages, and of faithful Christian folks we know today.

I have a young friend named Tammy who is living this Jesus-style dramatically. She was converted while a student at the University of Georgia. She then arrived as a student at Asbury Seminary with only enough money to take her through the first semester. Her story is a modern miracle of faith. She worked as much as she could, but there was no way she could work enough to pay her tuition and living expenses. So, she prayed. She never asked for money, but time and again, when she had nothing, no money to continue, somehow it would come.

The summer before her last year in seminary she went to India on a short-term mission and fell in love with all the children on the streets, many of them homeless. By a series of circumstances and following God's call, she returned to India a year later to establish Grace House, a home for abandoned or orphaned children. When I last heard from Tammy, there were sixty children under her care in two different facilities. The story is the same as it had been during her years in seminary: she is totally dependent upon the Lord. I have never known her to ask anyone for money, but miraculously, she receives what she needs.

She is an incarnation of the fact that discipline is to liberate us—to free us from, rather than sentence us to bondage. I regularly receive messages from her that confirm Richard Foster's claim noted last week:

Joy is the keynote of all the Disciplines. The purpose of the Disciplines is liberation from the stifling slavery to self-interest and fear. When the inner spirit is liberated from all that weighs it down, it can hardly be described as dull drudgery. Singing, dancing, and even shouting characterize the Disciplines of the spiritual life.[4]

Tammy has been serving in India for more than two decades, and she can now celebrate the marriage of children she rescued from the streets and has shepherded all their lives. She rejoices with a couple who are taking up the mantle of spiritual discipline and discipleship as they open a coffee shop to be a Christian social presence which enables them to share their discipleship witness.

Reflecting and Recording

Nothing is more important in our walking in the ways of God than Scripture. Memorizing and reflecting on Scripture is vital. Read Paul's testimony over and over, memorizing it if possible. No personal witness expresses the purpose of our walking in those ways better than Paul's:

> I have been crucified with Christ and I no longer live, but Christ lives in me. The life I now live in the body, I live by faith in the Son of God, who loved me and gave himself for me. (Gal. 2:20)

During the Day

If you have not yet memorized Paul's testimony, write it on a card and read it at different times throughout the day, reflecting on this question: To what degree can I make Paul's confession my own?

Children of the Day

But you, brothers and sisters, are not in darkness so that this day should surprise you like a thief. You are all children of the light and children of the day. We do not belong to the night or to the darkness. So then, let us not be like others, who are asleep, but let us be awake and sober. For those who sleep, sleep at night, and those who get drunk, get drunk at night. But since we belong to the day, let us be sober, putting on faith and love as a breastplate, and the hope of salvation as a helmet. For God did not appoint us to suffer wrath but to receive salvation through our Lord Jesus Christ. He died for us so that, whether we are awake or asleep, we may live together with him. Therefore encourage one another and build each other up, just as in fact you are doing.

—1 Thess. 5:4–11

If the differences between a Christian and a non-Christian are not obvious, something is wrong—seriously wrong. In his epistle to the Thessalonians, Paul made a pointed distinction between those who belong to the day and those who belong to the night. There is a sharp distinction between children of light and children of darkness.

We disciples of Jesus are children of the day. As Karl Heim wrote: "What Jesus wants is not admirers, but disciples—those who will conform their lives to his." Meister Eckhart, a thirteenth-century Dominican mystic, reiterated this idea when he said, "There are many who are willing to follow our Lord half way—but not the other half."

In writing about Thomas à Kempis's *The Imitation of Christ*, Douglas Steere said:

[It] not only recruits those who have been admirers. It would train and draw these disciples until they were willing to enter "the other half," the half where the easy charts and pocket maps vanish and where there are no return tickets available. It, too, would launch them out upon 70,000 fathoms of water where the foot can no longer touch bottom, where there is no longer any trusting God and keeping your powder dry, but where one must now trust God and take what comes one day at a time.[5]

It is "the other half," following our coming into the Christian life, that we are most concerned about in this study. The salvation Jesus provides is not limited to the forgiveness of sin; it also has the power to break sin's control over our lives. Thomas à Kempis expressed this in an attention-getting way:

Thou hast good cause to be ashamed in looking upon the life of Jesus Christ, seeing thou hast not as yet endeavored to conform thyself more unto him, though thou hast been a long time in the way of God.[6]

For a small income, a long journey is undertaken; for everlasting life, many will scarce once lift a foot from the ground.[7]

If thou wilt reign with Me, bear the cross with Me.

For only the servants of the cross can find the way of blessedness and of true light.[8]

Being earnest disciples—children of the day—means being conformed to the likeness of Christ, through a process that continues throughout the Christian's life.

Reflecting and Recording

In the space provided underneath each of the à Kempis quotes, translate his words into your own. As you do so, reflect on your own life in terms of how you are living "the other half."

During the Day

Be sensitive to occasions today when you might deliberately express your desire to continue living "the other half."

Dead to Sin

So you also should consider yourselves to be dead to the power of sin and alive to God through Christ Jesus.

Do not let sin control the way you live; do not give in to sinful desires. Do not let any part of your body become an instrument of evil to serve sin. Instead, give yourselves completely to God, for you were dead, but now you have new life. So use your whole body as an instrument to do what is right for the glory of God. Sin is no longer your master, for you no longer live under the requirements of the law. Instead, you live under the freedom of God's grace.

—Rom. 6:11–14 NLT

This scripture is an image-packed passage, powerful in its description of the radical transformation of Christian conversion. Though Paul's image of slavery is alien to our experience, we get the message. Paul is telling the Roman Christians that, before they were Christians, they were slaves to a master called sin. They had no choice. But now, because Christ paid the price to set them free, they have a completely new set of options for their behavior.

We need to practice his admonition: "consider yourselves to be dead to the power of sin." In every situation—no matter how powerfully attractive; no matter how frustrating, threatening, or painful—we can choose our response. If we consider ourselves dead to the power of sin, the indwelling Christ, into whose image we are being shaped, is our new Master. He does not hold us in chains, but binds us to him in love. We are still free to choose which master we want to obey; too often, we go back to our old master. Like me,

41

when you do that, you probably find yourself saying, "I was not myself." And we are right; we are not the persons God knows us to be.

Learning to submit to Christ's rule in our lives is the process of being a Christian, "walking in the ways of God." A critical dimension of this is obedience. Mistakenly, we too often think of this in regard to big things, when what is crucial is obedience in little things. Christian sanctification, living out the Christian life, is a matter of making daily choices with the help of the Holy Spirit.

I have not read the writings of any saint who didn't argue that the secret of spiritual growth is obedience to God in little things. François Fénelon talked a great deal about faithfulness in little things being an indication of our love of God. In one passage he contrasted this with our inclination to think of great sacrifices as the heart of Christian devotion:

> Great virtues are rare, the opportunities for exercising them occur but seldom. When they present themselves we have been prepared before-hand, and we are excited by the very sacrifice we are making; we are sustained either by the brilliance of our action in the eyes of others, or by our own satisfaction in making so unusual an effort. But the opportunities for little sacrifices are unforeseen; they occur hourly; they constantly oblige us to struggle with our pride, with our indolence, with our hastiness or our discontent. If we would be truly faithful, nature can have no breathing time, she must die to all her own desires. People would far rather offer to God certain great sacrifices, however painful, provided they might still, in all lesser matters, follow their own tastes and inclinations. Nevertheless, it is by faithfulness in little things that the spirit of love and holiness is proved, and by which it can be distinguished from mere natural impulses.[9]

Reflecting and Recording

Spend a few minutes reflecting whether, and to what degree, you exercise considering yourself dead to sin.

Read Fénelon's words again, slowly and reflectively, questioning in what way his words are true in your life.

Specifically, in what way and to what degree is the following comment true in your life? "People would far rather offer to God certain great sacrifices, however painful, provided they might still, in all lesser matters, follow their own tastes and inclinations."

During the Day

As you move through the day, stay aware of how, by faithfulness in little things, the spirit of love and holiness is proved in your life.

Obedience in Love

Such "wisdom" does not come down from heaven but is earthly, unspiritual, demonic. For where you have envy and selfish ambition, there you find disorder and every evil practice.

But the wisdom that comes from heaven is first of all pure; then peace-loving, considerate, submissive, full of mercy and good fruit, impartial and sincere. Peacemakers who sow in peace reap a harvest of righteousness.

—James 3:15–18

Bernard of Clairvaux, a twelfth-century French saint, wrote a descriptive passage about the purifying fire of God, which burns within us to make us holy:

It is sent by God to arouse you and make you realize what you are in yourself, so that you may afterwards taste more sweetly what you are soon to become by the power of God. But the Fire which God is consuming indeed, but without causing pain; sweet is the burning, blissful devastation that its flames effect. For it is truly a "hot burning coal" but it acts like fire on our faults, only in order that it may act as unction to the soul.[10]

When I first read this passage, my mind fixated on the phrase "sweet is the burning." I had not heard the phrase, nor have I encountered it since. We simply do not connect fire with a personal experience we would consider sweet. Bernard could not have expressed it more powerfully.

The saints sought *purity of heart* because they knew that our actions spring from our hearts. Our sanctification and holiness involve the reformation of our hearts. Most of us know that, sooner or later, what is on our inside will express itself outwardly. This is one of the messages of the epistle of James. Concentrating on today's passage from James, Richard Foster observed:

If the central core of who we are is "earthly, unspiritual, devilish," what flows out will be "disorder and wickedness of every kind." Conversely, if the central core of who we are is "pure, peaceable, gentle, willing to yield, full of good fruits, without a trace of partiality or hypocrisy," then what flows out will be "a harvest of righteousness [which] is sown in peace for those who make peace."[11]

The divinely transformed heart produces right actions. Thus, an identifiable expression of holiness is a person's character. We need to keep reminding ourselves that God's command to God's people through Moses was: "Be holy because I, the LORD your God, am holy" (Lev. 19:2b). Peter repeated that command when he described how Christians are to live: "Just as he who called you is holy, so be holy in all you do; for it is written: 'Be holy, because I am holy'" (1 Peter 1:15–16).

The outcome of original sin is love of self. Martin Luther said: "In the Ten Commandments we see nothing else but self-love. . . . St. Augustine well says, 'The beginning of all sin is the love of one's own self . . .' Therefore, he lives best who lives not for himself, and he who lives for himself, lives worst."[12] With this fact dominating our lives, it is natural that some dramatic expression like fire would be used in thinking of the remedy.

In the Acts of the Apostles, Luke described the Holy Spirit coming as "tongues of fire" settling on the disciples (Acts 2:3). The fire that burns within us is the presence of the Holy Spirit, reforming our hearts to obedience and love. No wonder Bernard described it "sweet is the burning."

Reflecting and Recording

Read again, slowly and reflectively, Bernard's word about the sweet burning of fire within us. Then spend a few minutes examining your life in terms of the image of the Holy Spirit burning within you.

Is there a way that you might become more receptive and open to the Holy Spirit as a reforming fire?

During the Day

Images can assist us in the ongoing examination of our lives. Lodge the phrase "sweet is the burning" solidly in your mind. Yesterday you were invited to move through the day staying aware of how, by faithfulness in little things, the spirit of love and holiness is proved in your life. Continue that today with the present image of "sweet is the burning."

Pruning Time

Do you not know that in a race all the runners run, but only one gets the prize? Run in such a way as to get the prize. Everyone who competes in the games goes into strict training. They do it to get a crown that will not last, but we do it to get a crown that will last forever. Therefore I do not run like someone running aimlessly; I do not fight like a boxer beating the air. No, I strike a blow to my body and make it my slave so that after I have preached to others, I myself will not be disqualified for the prize.

—1 Cor. 9:24–27

I cringed when I first read the following paragraph. It still stings sharply every time I read it:

People do not drift toward Holiness. Apart from grace-driven effort, people do not gravitate toward godliness, prayer, obedience to Scripture, faith, and delight in the Lord. We drift toward compromise and call it tolerance; we drift toward disobedience and call it freedom; we drift toward superstition and call it faith. We cherish the indiscipline of lost self-control and call it relaxation; we slouch toward prayerlessness and delude ourselves into thinking we have escaped legalism; we slide toward godlessness and convince ourselves we have been liberated.[13]

I previously noted that if there is no obvious difference between Christians and non-Christians, then something is seriously wrong. Paul designated Christians as "children of the light" (1 Thess. 5:5), and he said that for no reason should children of light be confused with children of darkness. Even so, one of Paul's ongoing concerns—for himself and others—was the fact that the way back into the darkness is always open, and living in the light requires vigilance and discipline.

The Corinthians wanted to take the easy way, but Paul reminded them that no one can achieve anything of worth without the sternest self-discipline. In ancient Greece, the Isthmian Games, second only to the Olympic Games, took place in Corinth. The Corinthians could identify with Paul's fascination with the picture of the athlete. They knew the thrill of athletic contests. Paul reminded them of how intensely the athlete must train in order to compete and win. He also made the point that the athlete, for all his self-discipline and training, wins a crown of laurel leaves that withers within a few days, but the discipline of the Christian life results in a crown that lasts forever (eternal life).

Paul is dramatic: "I strike a blow to my body and make it my slave so that after I have preached to others, I myself will not be disqualified for the prize" (1 Cor. 9:27). In the history of the church, especially in the monastic movement, this notion of mortification suggested by Paul's testimony has been taken to extremes in the forms of beating themselves, starving themselves, or treating their bodies as enemies of spirituality, confusing Paul's warning about the flesh with the physical body and senses (Rom. 8:5–8). That's the reason I made the case on Day Two that holiness is primarily heart-work, bringing our wills in subjection to Christ's to conform our lives, faith, and desires to the desires of Jesus.

Even though mortification may have been distorted, even perverted, we must keep Paul's advice to remain alert and self-controlled predominant in our awareness. Many Christians have become casualties to casualness and carelessness. Our enemy, Satan, constantly seeks to penetrate our souls' defenses, which makes vigilance essential.

But discipline and vigilance alone are not enough. The saints talked a lot about pruning. Bernard of Clairvaux wrote:

Lord Jesus, how few souls there are who want to follow Thee! Everyone wants to reach Thee in the end because they know that "at Thy right hand are pleasures forevermore." They want the happiness that Thou canst give but not to imitate

Thee; they want to reign with Thee, but not to suffer. Even the carnal minded would like a holy death although they cannot stand a holy life. He says moreover, "the time of running has come." . . . I would point out also that, where your soul is concerned, it is no good pruning only once; you must do it often always, if possible. For, if you are honest with yourself, there will always be something that needs cutting back; for whatever progress you make while you are still in the body, you are mistaken if you think your faults are dead, rather than merely repressed. . . . In view of this great danger, I can only advise you to watch yourself most carefully and to cut away all offending growths as soon as they appear. For virtues and vices cannot grow together; if your virtues are to grow, your faults must be prevented from making any development at all. So it is always pruning time with us, brethren, because there is always need for it.[14]

Reflecting and Recording

Saint Francis de Sales used the imagery of incision and circumcision to challenge us in our pruning: "The greater part of Christians usually practice incision instead of circumcision. They will make a cut indeed in a diseased part; but as for employing the knife of circumcision, to take away whatever is superfluous from the heart, few go so far."[15]

Focusing on that image, how willing are you "to take away whatever is superfluous from the heart"? Make some notes about what needs to be taken away from your heart.

During the Day

Seek someone today who is willing to discuss discipline in your common Christian walk. Be prepared to talk about the necessity of incision.

Perfection in Love

Not that I have already obtained this or have already reached the goal; but I press on to make it my own, because Christ Jesus has made me his own. Beloved, I do not consider that I have made it my own; but this one thing I do: forgetting what lies behind and straining forward to what lies ahead, I press on toward the goal for the prize of the heavenly call of God in Christ Jesus. Let those of us then who are mature be of the same mind; and if you think differently about anything, this too God will reveal to you. Only let us hold fast to what we have attained.

Brothers and sisters, join in imitating me, and observe those who live according to the example you have in us.

—Phil. 3:12–17 NRSV

A feature newspaper article entitled "The Morning After" described how it really feels to play pro football every Sunday. These were the first paragraphs:

Monday mornings are the toughest for Jerome Bettis. Shortly after 9 o'clock, the Pittsburgh Steelers running back awakens and can barely move his neck. One of his ankles is purple and swollen. His left hip still hurts. His ribs sting at even the lightest touch. There is a piercing sensation in his lower back. His shoulders, he says, "feel like they are on fire."

He begins the laborious process of getting out of bed, shimmying to the mattress' edge and gingerly lowering his sore feet to the floor. He rests there for a few minutes, feeling his blood start to circulate.

Usually, he hoists himself upright and limps slowly to the bathroom. On the rough days, there is an additional challenge: the stairs from the second floor of his immaculate home to the first. At the edge of the first step, he sometimes has no choice but to have a seat, then either carefully slide himself down, one excruciating step at a time, or literally crawl until he has reached the ground level.[16]

Jarrett Bell, writer of the article, went on to describe Jerome Bettis's following week:

By midafternoon Monday, Bettis had received treatment, including electrical stimulation and ice. He rode his stationary bike for twenty minutes, then walked on a treadmill for another twenty. That was Monday. During the week Bettis would ride his bike each day for forty-five minutes. He had one-hour, full-body massages on Tuesdays and Thursdays. Daily team practices were complemented by weightlifting sessions, and he was in the training room daily.

"Everybody sees us on Sundays," Bettis said, stretching his limbs on the floor of his spacious family room Monday afternoon. "But if people saw us on Monday through Saturday and got a sense of the toll this can take on your body, they would really understand that we love this game 10 times more than they imagined."

"You definitely need to stay motivated because it can be easy to be demoralized. Especially if your team's not doing well. It can be tough to get up on Mondays, thinking about getting yourself ready for the next week."[17]

When I read this story, I cut it out of the newspaper, and put it in a file for illustration in talking about discipline and discipleship. As Romans 8:13 states, Christians are to "mortify the deeds of the body" of our evil nature (KJV), or as another translation says, we are to "put to death the deeds of the body" (NRSV). While putting to death these deeds requires discipline, renunciation, and vigilance, a rigid adherence to rules and regulations leads to dismal, joyless perfectionism.

Sanctifying grace, which leads to holiness, just like justifying grace, is utterly and completely a work of undeserved grace. John Wesley traced the process:

From the time of our being born again, the gradual work of sanctification takes place. We are enabled "by the Spirit" to "mortify the deeds of the body" of our evil nature; and as we are more and more dead to sin, we are more and more alive to God. We go on from grace to grace.

It is thus that we wait for entire sanctification; for a "full" salvation from all our sins—from pride, self-will, anger, unbelief; or, as the apostle expressed it, "go on unto perfection."

But what is perfection? The word has various senses. Here it means perfect love. It is love excluding sin; love filling the heart, taking up the whole capacity of the soul. It is love "rejoicing evermore, praying without ceasing, in everything giving thanks."[18]

This was no empty claim. We have not given enough attention to the vast number of saints who thirsted for this perfection/holiness and claimed it. Read today's scripture again. Paul not only lived what he taught, he taught the Philippians to imitate him, "and observe those who live according to the example you have in us" (Phil. 3:17 NRSV).

As we press on toward holiness, we must guard against the pitfall of connecting holiness with works/righteousness. We strive "to enter in" (see Luke 13:24 KJV) as Jesus calls us, but our striving is not "works" that we have to do to earn merit; our striving is kept connected to grace (see Ephesians 2:8–9). We use all the classical spiritual disciplines and means of grace (we will be focusing on those in the coming days) not for merit or as virtue, but as a way to place ourselves before God to reform our hearts, shape our character, and empower us for kingdom living.

Reflecting and Recording

God does not seek to improve us but to radically *transform* us. C. S. Lewis was adamant in the expression of this truth: "The goal towards which [God] is beginning to guide you is absolute perfection; and no power in the whole universe, except you yourself, can prevent him from taking you to that goal."[19]

Do you believe Lewis's claim? Reflect on your Christian pilgrimage. Have you practiced the faith as though you believed in the possibility of perfection?

Assuming you believe Lewis's claim, write a prayer that expresses your conviction, desire, and willingness to yield to God and allow God to accomplish the divine will for your holiness.

During the Day

Choose two or three times during this day (at meal times, waiting for an appointment, during a break from work, etc.) that you will pray the prayer you just wrote.

WEEK TWO
Group Sharing

Introduction

Participation in a group such as this is a covenant relationship. You will profit most as you keep the daily discipline of reading and using this study guide, and as you faithfully attend these weekly meetings. Do not feel guilty if you have to miss a day in the study, or be discouraged if you are not able to give the full thirty minutes in daily discipline. Don't hesitate to share that with the group.

Our growth, in part, hinges upon our group participation, so share as openly and honestly as you can. Listen to what persons are saying. Sometimes there is meaning beyond the surface of their words that you may pick up if you are really attentive.

Being a sensitive participant in this fashion is crucial. Responding immediately to the feelings we pick up is also crucial. Sometimes it is important for the group to focus its entire attention upon a particular individual. If some need or concern is expressed, it may be appropriate for the leader to ask the group to enter into a brief period of special prayer for the person or concerns revealed.

Participants should not always depend upon the leader for this kind of sensitivity, for the leader may miss it. Even if you aren't the leader, don't hesitate to ask the group to join you in special prayer. This praying may be silent, or someone may wish to lead the group in prayer.

Remember, you have a contribution to make to the group. What you consider trivial or unimportant may be just what another person needs to hear. We are not seeking to be profound but to share our experience.

Sharing Together

Note that, in any given week, it may not be possible in your allotted time frame to use all the suggestions provided. The leader should select what will be most beneficial to the group. It is important that the leader be thoroughly familiar with these suggestions in order to move through them selectively according to the time available. The leader should plan, but do not hesitate to change the plan according to the nature of the sharing taking place and the questions and needs that emerge.

1. Open your sharing time together with the leader offering a brief prayer of thanksgiving for the opportunity of sharing with the group and petitions for openness in sharing and loving response to each other.
2. Invite each person to share his or her most meaningful day of the study so far. The leader should begin and model sharing by telling why a particular day was meaningful.
3. Next, invite each person to share their most interesting or difficult day, with the reasons why.

Praying Together

Hopefully, you have the names of the persons in the group. The effectiveness of this group and the quality of relationships is enhanced by a commitment to pray for each other by name each day. Pray for each person daily, remembering how they may have shared in the group, and what you have come to know about them and their families.

1. If the group (or two or three in the group) are familiar with it, begin your prayer time singing "Breathe on Me, Breath of God":

> Breathe on me, breath of God,
> Fill me with life anew,
> That I may love what Thou dost love,
> And do what Thou wouldst do.[20]

2. Invite persons to share needs within their own life, the congregation, or community. When the sharing is done, have a time of silent prayer responding to the requests that have been made, then invite two or three persons to offer prayer on behalf of the group in response to the needs shared.

Twila & Ray
Lucia
Marlene
David Staton
Adrienne - cataract

Week Three
Growth in Grace

No Quick Way to Be a Saint

Then Jesus told his disciples, "If any want to become my followers, let them deny themselves and take up their cross and follow me. For those who want to save their life will lose it, and those who lose their life for my sake will find it. For what will it profit them if they gain the whole world but forfeit their life? Or what will they give in return for their life?"

—Matt. 16:24–26 NRSV

All of us could recall the events and crucial times in our ministry which were watershed occasions, transition times, marking dramatic redirection or paradigm shifts in our understanding of vocation, church, the Christian life, and spirituality. One of those came for me when I was invited to join the staff of The Upper Room to direct a ministry primarily calling people to a life of prayer, providing direction and resources for growth in the practice of prayer, and giving structure to a united expression of prayer by people around the world. I told Dr. Wilson Weldon, then editor of The Upper Room, that the fact the board was inviting me to assume this responsibility showed the church to be in desperate straits, since I was such a novice in this area of life and its development.

This responsibility forced me to be even more deliberate and disciplined in my own personal life, but also introduced me to a wider dimension of spirituality than I had known. I became intensely interested in the great devotional classics. The Upper Room had published a collection of little booklets, selections from the great spiritual writings of the ages, writers whose names I barely knew and to whose writings I was a stranger: Julian of Norwich, William Law, François Fénelon, Francis of Assisi, Evelyn Underhill, Brother Lawrence, and an array of others. I began a deliberate practice of keeping company with the saints, seeking to immerse myself in the writings of these folks which have endured through the centuries, expressing Christian faith in life and becoming classic resources for the Christian pilgrimage.

I have already referred to and quoted some of these persons as resources for our journey in Christ. You will be introduced to others as we continue our study.

As I have kept company with these saints, I've observed some characteristics they had in common:

they passionately sought the Lord;

they discovered a gracious God;

they took Scripture seriously;

Jesus was alive in their experience;

they practiced discipline, at the heart of which was prayer;

they didn't seek ecstasy but surrender of their will to the Lord;

they were thirsty for holiness;

they lived not for themselves but for God and for others; and

they knew joy and peace, transcending all circumstances.

Did you note? They practiced discipline, at the heart of which was prayer. The saints have all known that there is no quick way "to be a saint, and quickly." Saint Francis de Sales challenged us:

We must begin with a strong and constant resolution to give ourselves wholly to God, professing to Him, in a tender, loving manner, from the bottom of our hearts, that we intend to be His without any reserve, and then we must often go back and renew this same resolution.[1]

That's discipline, and a challenge to all would-be Christians. Anyone who has read the Gospels knows that Jesus' call is to a "narrow" way (see Matthew 7:13–14). He could not have made it clearer than when he told his disciples: "Whoever wants to be my disciple must deny themselves and take up their cross and follow me" (Matt. 16:24). Paul also made it scathingly clear: "I appeal to you therefore, brothers and sisters, by the mercies of God, to present your bodies as a living sacrifice, holy and acceptable to God, which is your spiritual worship" (Rom. 12:1 NRSV).

I don't know a Christian in all the ages to whom we turn for teaching and inspiration who did not give himself or herself consistently to discipline and devotion. In his book *The Road Less Traveled*, psychiatrist Scott Peck observed:

> There are many people I know who possess a vision of personal evolution yet seem to lack the will for it. They want, and believe it is possible, to skip over the discipline, to find an easy shortcut to sainthood. Often they attempt to attain it by simply imitating the superficialities of saints, retiring to the desert or taking up carpentry. Some even believe that by such imitation they have really become saints and prophets, and are unable to acknowledge that they are still children and face the painful fact that they must start at the beginning and go through the middle.[2]

The beginning is, as de Sales said, "a strong and constant resolution to give ourselves wholly to God" and the *middle* consists of often going back to renew this same resolution.

Reflecting and Recording

Read again the characteristics of the saints I listed. Put a plus (+) by those that are reflected at some level in your life. Reflect on the list again, and put a double plus (++) by ones you need and want to work on.

During the Day

As you move through the day, notice the discipline quotient of people around you. Observe how much discipline a particular job requires, or think about how disciplined certain individuals had to be to reach their positions in their work or avocation. Talk to one or two persons about the importance of discipline in their lives and yours.

My All in All

Oh, the depth of the riches of the wisdom and knowledge of God!
How unsearchable his judgments,
and his paths beyond tracing out!
"Who has known the mind of the Lord?
Or who has been his counselor?"
"Who has ever given to God,
that God should repay them?"
For from him and through him and for him are all things.
To him be the glory forever! Amen.

—Rom. 11:33–36

In his landmark work *Streams of Living Water*, Richard Foster examined six dimensions of faith and practice that define Christian tradition, which he called "streams," or "traditions." He identified them as: (1) contemplative, (2) holiness, (3) charismatic, (4) social justice, (5) evangelical, and (6) incarnational. These traditions span Christian history; they overlap in time, but have specific periods of flowering.

Interestingly, it is difficult to position present-day Methodist/Wesleyan expressions in a singular tradition. Some would say we are in the evangelical tradition; others, the holiness tradition; and, at our best, we have reflected the social justice tradition.

The holiness stream of Christian life and faith "focuses upon the inward reformation of the heart and the development of 'holy habits.' We can rely upon these deeply ingrained habits of virtue to make our lives function appropriately and to bring forth substantial character formation."[3]

Foster pointed to Phoebe Palmer as an inspiring and defining example of this holiness stream. She was an extraordinary teacher, passionate in her concern for humanity, and a powerful preacher of the holiness way. Charles Edward White said Palmer might well be "the most influential female theologian the Church has yet produced."[4] She was born in 1807 and lived until 1874. Her father was a young convert of John Wesley, so the history and teachings of prominent Methodist leaders dominated the family's religious life. She married a physician, and they had six children. The third child, Eliza, died in an especially tragic accident; the family's maid dropped a burning oil lamp on the gauze curtain covering the baby's crib, burning her to death. That loss was a life-changing point for Phoebe. She turned to the Bible and to God. She later testified:

While pacing the room, crying to God, amid the tumult of grief, my mind was arrested by a gentle whisper, saying, "Your Heavenly Father loves you. He would not permit such a great trial, without intending that some great good, proportionate in magnitude and weight should result. . . ."

In the agony of my soul I had exclaimed, "O, what shall I do!" And the answer now came,—"Be still, and know that I am God." I took up the precious WORD, and cried, "O, teach me the lesson of this trial," and the first lines to catch my eye on opening the Bible, were these, "O, the depth of the riches, both of the wisdom and knowledge of God! How unsearchable are his judgments and his ways past finding out!"

. . . The tumult of feeling was hushed. . . . "What thou knowest not now, thou shalt know hereafter," was assuringly whispered. Wholly subdued before the Lord, my chastened spirit nestled in quietness under the wing of the Holy Comforter.

. . . And now I have resolved, that . . . the time I would have devoted to her, shall be spent in work for Jesus. And if diligent and self-sacrificing in carrying out my resolve, the death of this child may result in the spiritual life of many.[5]

This dramatic, ecstatic event gave Palmer an unquenchable zeal for the work of Christ. She developed and taught the rest of her life what she called "altar theology." According to this theology, as Christians, our altar is Christ. Upon this altar we offer ourselves as sacrifices. Palmer taught: "Since everything that touches the altar is holy, we are holy. We are holy when we place everything we are upon the altar. We therefore live in a state of holiness and sanctification as we continually give ourselves as a living sacrifice to Christ, our altar."[6]

Phoebe Palmer and many others contended that there is no holiness apart from our being on the altar:

There is therefore no sanctity, if thou, O Lord, withdraw thine hand.

No wisdom availeth, if thou cease to guide.

No courage helpeth, if thou leave off to defend.

No chastity is secure, if thou do not protect it.

No custody of our own availeth, if thy sacred watchfulness be not present with us.

For, if we be left [of thee] we sink and perish; but being visited [of thee] we are
    raised up and live.

Truly we are inconstant, but by thee we are confirmed: we wax cold, but by thee we
    are inflamed. . . . Shall the clay glory against him that formeth it?[7]

Reflecting and Recording

Has there been a time in your Christian pilgrimage (maybe not as dramatic as Phoebe Palmer's) when you realized you must lay your life on the altar of Christ and become a living sacrifice for him? Make some notes here to describe that experience.

Spend some time reflecting on Palmer's claim, "We are holy when we place everything we are upon the altar."

During the Day

Many hymns employ Phoebe Palmer's altar theology, especially gospel hymns written during the holiness revival of which Palmer was a part. One of these was "I Surrender All." If you know this hymn, and are in a place where you can do so, sing it now. If you don't know the words, write them on a card to carry with you, and find occasion to either sing or repeat the words as an altar commitment:

All to Jesus I surrender,
All to Him I freely give;
I will ever love and trust Him,
In His presence daily live.
I surrender all, I surrender all;
All to Thee, my blessed Savior,
I surrender all.[8]

We Cannot Control the Spirit

In the year that King Uzziah died, I saw the Lord, high and exalted, seated on a throne; and the train of his robe filled the temple. Above him were seraphim, each with six wings: With two wings they covered their faces, with two they covered their feet, and with two they were flying. And they were calling to one another:

"Holy, holy, holy is the Lord Almighty;

the whole earth is full of his glory."

At the sound of their voices the doorposts and thresholds shook and the temple was filled with smoke.

"Woe to me!" I cried. "I am ruined! For I am a man of unclean lips, and I live among a people of unclean lips, and my eyes have seen the King, the Lord Almighty."

Then one of the seraphim flew to me with a live coal in his hand, which he had taken with tongs from the altar. With it he touched my mouth and said, "See, this has touched your lips; your guilt is taken away and your sin atoned for."

—Isa. 6:1–7

As I have kept company with the saints through the years, all have witnessed to the vivid presence of the Holy Spirit. The Holy Spirit's power was demonstrated strikingly in their lives, and many often had ecstatic experiences. We always need to remember that the important issue is the presence of God, not how that presence is made known.

Jean-Pierre de Caussade spoke of how one must forget everything else and think only of God. Sometimes as this happens, a person may pass entire days without thinking of anything else, "as though one had become quite stupid." He continued:

It often happens that God even places certain souls in this state, which is called the emptiness of the spirit and of the understanding, or the state of nothingness. The annihilation of one's own spirit wonderfully prepares the soul for the reception of that of Jesus Christ. This is the mystical death to the working of one's own activity, and renders the soul capable of undergoing the divine operation.[9]

This "mystical death" is what Jesus was talking about when he called us to "deny" ourselves (Matt. 16:24). We considered this on Day Four last week when we reflected on considering ourselves "dead to sin" (Rom. 6:11). It is the rhythm of the Christian life: dying and rising with Christ (see Colossians 3:3–4).

As indicated yesterday, Richard Foster identified a charismatic tradition in the history of Christian faith and practice that is relevant to de Caussade's claim. The tradition gives special attention to the work of the Holy Spirit and abounds with charismatic, ecstatic experience. Foster identified the life and ministry of Saint Francis of Assisi as a historical paradigm for the charismatic tradition. He identified the Azusa Street Revival in the early 1900s as a contemporary paradigm of the charismatic tradition. Many of the present-day Charismatic/Pentecostal movements grew out of that revival. C. H. Mason, founder of the Church of God in Christ, was one of many African-American Pentecostal leaders whose defining experience of the Holy Spirit was in the Azusa Street Mission. He testified of that experience:

The Spirit came upon the saints and upon me . . . Then I gave up for the Lord to have His way within me. So there came a wave of Glory into me and all of my being was filled with the Glory of the Lord. So when He had gotten me straight on my feet, there came a light which enveloped my entire being above the brightness of the sun. When I opened my mouth to say "Glory," a flame touched my tongue which ran down to me. My language changed and no word could I speak in my own tongue. Oh! I was filled with the Glory of the Lord. My soul was then satisfied.[10]

Doesn't that sound like Isaiah's witness in today's scripture? Read that passage again. We need to thank God that all our attempts to control or manage the Holy Spirit ultimately fail. Why can't we accept that, as the saints have taught us, and joyfully surrender to the Spirit's leading, moving from day to day, open and expectant that God will surprise us with an outbreaking of the Spirit as we have not yet imagined?

Reflecting and Recording

How do you respond to de Caussade's phrase, "the annihilation of one's own spirit"? Are you turned off by that phrase? Live with this question for a minute.

Did de Caussade's words, the "mystical death to the working of one's own activity" register for you as his explanation of "the annihilation of one's own spirit"?

Write a brief prayer expressing your desire and willingness to die to the working of your own activity in order for the Holy Spirit to work in your life.

During the Day

Seek to deliberately acknowledge and cultivate God's presence in what you see, in the persons you meet, and especially in your conversations.

Submission Is a Love Word

Now there was a Pharisee, a man named Nicodemus who was a member of the Jewish ruling council. He came to Jesus at night and said, "Rabbi, we know that you are a teacher who has come from God. For no one could perform the signs you are doing if God were not with him."

Jesus replied, "Very truly I tell you, no one can see the kingdom of God unless they are born again."

"How can someone be born when they are old?" Nicodemus asked. "Surely they cannot enter a second time into their mother's womb to be born!"

Jesus answered, "Very truly I tell you, no one can enter the kingdom of God unless they are born of water and the Spirit. Flesh gives birth to flesh, but the Spirit gives birth to spirit. You should not be surprised at my saying, 'You must be born again.'"

—John 3:1–7

In *The Cloister Walk*, Kathleen Norris describes how she became a Benedictine oblate. She said she knew two things: (1) she didn't feel ready to become an oblate, but she had to act, to take the plunge; and (2) she had no idea where doing so would lead.

"An oblation is an abbreviated yet powerful profession of monastic vows." The oblate attaches himself/herself to a particular monastery by signing a document on the altar during Mass, promising to follow the Rule of Saint Benedict insofar as his/her situation will allow.[11] Norris confessed:

The fact that I'd been raised a thorough Protestant, with little knowledge of religious orders, and no sense of monasticism as a living tradition, was less an obstacle to my becoming an oblate than the many doubts about the Christian religion that had been with me since my teens. Still, although I had little sense of where I'd been, I knew that standing before the altar in a monastery chapel was a remarkable place for one to be, and making an oblation was a remarkable, if not incomprehensible, thing for me to be doing.

The Word "oblate" is from the Latin for "to offer," and Jesus himself is often referred to as an "oblation" in the literature of the early church. Many people now translate "oblate" as "associate," and while that may seem to describe the relationship modern oblates have with monastic communities, it does not adequately convey the religious dimension of being an oblate. Substituting the word "associate" for "oblation" in reference to Jesus demonstrates this all too well; no longer an offering, Jesus becomes a junior partner in a law firm. The ancient word "oblate" proved instructive for me. Having no idea what it meant, I appreciated its rich history when I first looked it up in the dictionary. But I also felt it presumptuous to claim to be an "offering" and was extremely reluctant to apply to myself a word that had so often been applied to Jesus Christ.[12]

After making that confession, Norris told about the monk who was to be her oblate director, that is, the one who guided her studies of the Rule, "a period that was supposed to last a year but rambled on for nearly three." She spoke appreciatively of this spiritual guide. One day she said to him: "'I can't imagine why God would want me, of all people, as an offering. But if God is foolish enough to take me as I am, I guess I'd better do it.' The monk smiled broadly and said, 'You're ready.'"[13]

That kind of submission is the topic of this week's readings. Again, looking at the saints, they did not seek ecstasy, but surrender to God. They knew that in the Bible, *submission* is a love word, not a control word. It means letting another love, teach, influence, and shape you. On the human level, the degree to which we submit to others is the degree to which we will experience their love. Regardless of how much love another person has for us, we cannot appropriate that love unless we are open, vulnerable, and submissive.

The saints experienced the same thing in relation to God. They knew that it is only when we can imagine what God wants with us, or what God might do with us—and certainly when we are humble enough to know that anything God does for us or with us is all grace—only then, can we put ourselves in the position for the Holy Spirit to work within us.

Perhaps the best-known teaching about this topic in the New Testament is the story of Nicodemus. The language of "being born again" suggests something dramatic, but we must not allow that to cause us to question our experience. As John Wesley suggested:

> There is an irreconcilable variability in the operations of the Holy Spirit on the souls of men; more especially as to the manner of justification. Many find Him rushing upon them like a torrent, while they experience
>
> "The overwhelming power of saving grace."
>
> This has been the experience of many . . . But in others he works in a very different way.
>
> "He deigns his influence to infuse,
> Sweet, refreshing, as the violet dews."[14]

The way the Spirit works in our life is not our decision; being open to his work is. The prayer of our heart is that of the hymn, "Mold me and make me after Thy will."[15]

Reflecting and Recording

Consider the occasion or process of your becoming a professing Christian. Would you describe your conversion as a time of the Holy Spirit's "rushing upon [you] like a torrent," as you experienced the overwhelming power of saving grace? Or would your experience more aptly be described: "He deigns his influence to infuse, Sweet, refreshing, as the violet dews"?

Seek to get in touch with that experience. Make some notes describing your thoughts and feelings. How much ecstasy did you experience? Did you think in terms of submission and surrender?

If, like Kathleen Norris, you shared what you have thought and written about your coming into the Christian life with a spiritual guide would he or she say "you're ready" to journey on to sanctification?

During the Day

If you don't know the following hymn prayer, copy and carry it with you. Make this your prayer today and for a few days:

Mold me and make me after Thy will,
While I am waiting, yielded and still.[16]

God's Grace and Our Efforts

I ask then: Did God reject his people? By no means! I am an Israelite myself, a descendant of Abraham, from the tribe of Benjamin. God did not reject his people, whom he foreknew. Don't you know what Scripture says in the passage about Elijah—how he appealed to God against Israel: "Lord, they have killed your prophets and torn down your altars; I am the only one left, and they are trying to kill me"? And what was God's answer to him? "I have reserved for myself seven thousand who have not bowed the knee to Baal." So too, at the present time there is a remnant chosen by grace. And if by grace, then it cannot be based on works; if it were, grace would no longer be grace.

—Rom. 11:1–6

We have noted more than once that if the differences between a Christian and a non-Christian are not obvious, something is seriously wrong. We have also warned against thinking our performance leads to, or is a sign of, holiness. John Wesley's most important contribution to theology and understanding the Christian life was maintaining the dynamic between God's work of grace in our lives, and our own efforts to live in response to this grace.

There's a wonderful old story about a church in Ystad, Sweden. Back in 1716, King Charles XII announced to that little town that he was going to come and visit them, and that he would worship in the village church. The pastor of the church got all excited about the presence of the king in his congregation. He put aside the prescribed text for that Sunday and, instead, delivered a sermon in the form of a eulogy on the greatness of the royal family.

Three months later, a gift arrived at the church in a big box. The pastor was thrilled; it was a present from the king. But he wasn't ready for that particular present. Inside the box was a life-size crucifix, a life-like statue of Jesus on the cross, with this instruction: "Place this on the pillar opposite the pulpit, so that the one who stands in the pulpit to preach will always be reminded of his proper subject."

That is the bottom line, not just in our preaching, but in our total life. Christ gave himself to us in death on the cross for salvation, justifying us by grace through faith. That's the proper subject of our salvation. As we stay alive in gratitude to that, works of justice and mercy flow from us, even works of which we are not capable. We are empowered by the Holy Spirit.

Later, in Week Seven, we will consider the fact that we act our way into Christlikeness. That is not acting our way into being justified, but acting like Christ in gratitude for his saving love.

Jerry, my wife, and I feel we have the need to be reminded of this, so there are printed words posted in places where we are most likely to notice them. On our coffee maker is this neatly printed reminder: "The glory of God is us fully alive in Christ." On the space to the left of the door as we leave our bathroom is a copy of the popular contemporary gospel song "In Christ Alone." Occasionally, when I am anticipating a tough day, I will read all the words of that song, sometimes even singing a part of it.

Not just printed words, but paintings and art pieces are our constant reminders. On the wall before me, at the desk where I am writing, there is a beautifully carved wooden cross. We have a Sadao Watanabe print of *The Wise and Foolish Virgins*, which reminds us to be prepared, and my wife's painting, *Grace*, which is a powerful reminder of unmerited grace, God seeking us even before we seek him.

Reflecting and Recording

How are you at remembering? Do you need to establish some reminders in places in your home and work that will easily get your attention?

During the Day

Think about your need for reminders as you move through the day. Select a couple of things that might be easy to access and put in good reminder places in your home.

Attention and Affirmation

A leper came to him begging him, and kneeling he said to him, "If you choose, you can make me clean." Moved with pity, Jesus stretched out his hand and touched him, and said to him, "I do choose. Be made clean!" immediately the leprosy left him, and he was made clean. After sternly warning him he sent him away at once, saying to him, "See that you say nothing to anyone; but go, show yourself to the priest, and offer for your cleansing what Moses commanded, as a testimony to them." But he went out and began to proclaim it freely, and to spread the word, so that Jesus could no longer go into a town openly, but stayed out in the country; and people came to him from every quarter.

—Mark 1:40–45 NRSV

Those who are unhappy have no need for anything in this world but people capable of giving them their attention. The capacity to give one's attention to a sufferer is a very rare and difficult thing; it is almost a miracle; it *is* a miracle. Nearly all those who think they have this capacity do not possess it. Warmth of heart, impulsiveness, pity are not enough. . . .

The love of our neighbor in all its fullness simply means being able to say to him [or her]: "What are you going through?"[17]

This word of Simone Weil, the French mystic, sounds a challenging call to generosity of life. The call is to give our attention to others. Time and attention go together. But the truth is: we can give people our time without giving them our attention.

In the first chapter of his Gospel, Mark told the story of Jesus' forty days in the wilderness, his call and baptism, then his call of the disciples, and his beginning ministry. He recorded a series of healings, one of which was of a leper.

In New Testament times leprosy was the most dreaded of all diseases. The victim not only suffered physical debilitation, but also mental and emotional pain and anguish. Lepers were forced to live alone, and they had to wear special clothing so others could identify and avoid them. Perhaps the most abysmal humiliation was that they were required by law to announce their despicable condition: "Unclean!"

Mark told of one of these lepers coming boldly to Jesus, kneeling before him, and appealing, "If you want to, you can make me clean" (Mark 1:40 PHILLIPS). Then, there was packed into one beautiful sentence almost everything Jesus was and is about: "Jesus was filled with pity for him, and stretched out his hand and placed it on the leper, saying, 'Of course I want to—be clean!'" (v. 41 PHILLIPS). That tells it all.

Seek the full impact of this experience. By law, the leper had no right to even draw near Jesus, much less speak to him. How we do not know, but the leper knew that, despite his repulsive disease and his grotesque appearance, Jesus would see him, really see him, and respond to him as a person. Notice Jesus' response: he listened; he looked at him; and he touched him—the three action responses that no one else would dare make to a leper.

Jesus listened to the leper. Is there anything that enhances our feelings of worth more than being listened to? When you listen to me you say, "I value you. You are important. I will hear what you say."

Jesus looked at him and gave the leper his attention. What that must have meant for the leper! He knew he meant something to someone. It is an affirming relationship; a person in his or her wholeness wholly attending another person.

Simone Weil continued the word with which we began today with some clear teaching about how we look at another:

. . . it is indispensable, to know how to look at him [or her] in a certain way.

This way of looking is first of all attentive. The soul empties itself of all its own contents in order to receive into itself the being it is looking at, just as he [or she] is, in all his [or her] truth.

Only [the one] who is capable of attention can do this.[18]

Jesus not only looked and listened to the leper, he touched the leper. To be generous with our attention, we cannot remain aloof; we must deliberately reach out, touch, and become involved.

When I give attention by looking, listening, and touching, the Spirit comes alive in relationship. When I listen and look with mind and heart, revelation comes; the gap between the other person and me is bridged. Sensitivity comes that is not my own. I feel the pain, frustration, and anguish of the other. Beyond myself and my own resources, I become an instrument of miracle-working love.

Healing, comfort, reconciliation, strength, and guidance come to others when we generously give them our attention by looking, listening, and touching.

Reflecting and Recording

Make the decision now that you are going to practice listening and looking in all your relationships. Begin in your most intimate settings with your family and your closest friends. But don't stop there. To be truly generous with your attention, you must give it to all whose lives intersect with yours. Pray for insight and for the will to follow through with this practice.

During the Day

Return for a moment to Simone Weil's words: "Warmth of heart, impulsiveness, pity are not enough." To make our generosity of attention count the most, we need to know how to look and listen.

"The soul empties itself of all its own contents in order to receive into itself the being it is looking at, just as he [or she] is, in all his [or her] truth." This means we must give our attention *prayerfully*.

Contemplate these statements in relation to persons you will be meeting today.

Obedience Is Absolutely Essential

"Beware of false prophets, who come to you in sheep's clothing but inwardly are ravenous wolves. You will know them by their fruits. Are grapes gathered from thorns, or figs from thistles? In the same way, every good tree bears good fruit, but the bad tree bears bad fruit. A good tree cannot bear bad fruit, nor can a bad tree bear good fruit. Every tree that does not bear good fruit is cut down and thrown into the fire. Thus you will know them by their fruits.

"Not everyone who says to me, 'Lord, Lord,' will enter the kingdom of heaven, but only the one who does the will of my Father in heaven. On that day many will say to me, 'Lord, Lord, did we not prophesy in your name, and cast out demons in your name, and do many deeds of power in your name?' Then I will declare to them, 'I never knew you; go away from me, you evildoers.'"

—Matt. 7:15–23 NRSV

One of the characteristics of the saints with whom I have kept company is *they believed that obedience was absolutely essential* for spiritual life and growth. They took their cue from Jesus. We do have a right to ask, to seek, and to know the will of God, but once we know it, nothing but obedience will do. The saints sought to arrive at the place in their relationship to Christ that their one longing was to live and walk in a way that would please God and bring glory to God's name. Saint Francis de Sales insisted that attaining this goal is possible:

It is a great error of certain souls otherwise good and pious that they believe they cannot retain interior repose in the midst of business and perplexities. Surely there is no commotion greater than that of a vessel in the midst of the sea; yet those on board do not give up the thought of resting and sleeping, and the compass remains always in its place, turning towards the pole. Here is the point: we must be careful to keep the compass of our will in order, that it may never turn elsewhere than to the pole of the divine pleasure.[19]

But how do we know God's will? How do we keep the compass of our will in order? The first and primary condition is complete surrender and obedience, which fits us to receive instruction and guidance about God's will for us.

There are three seeds which, when planted in the soil of obedience, produce the fruit of God's will in our lives: (1) Scripture study; (2) conferencing—deliberately and honestly sharing with godly persons for edification and discernment of God's will and guidance (We will focus on these when we discuss each of them as a particular means of grace.); and (3) divine conviction, wrought by the Holy Spirit, must be pervasive in all we seek. As we discussed on Day Five of Week Two, the Holy Spirit reforms our hearts to obedience.

God has a *general* will for all of his people; God also has a *particular* will for each of us. Obedience is essential in discovering God's will, and there is only one textbook. Jesus is our model. With that pervasive in our minds, a special application of God's will concerning each of us personally comes through the Holy Spirit. There will be occasions when the Holy Spirit plants solidly in our minds certain convictions about God's will. We dare not quench the Spirit. Yet, it is altogether in keeping with God's direction that we test these, particularly through Scripture and Christian conferencing. Again, however, once we know God's will, nothing but obedience will do.

Reflecting and Recording

Recall and record here your clearest recollecting of knowing and obeying God's will.

Spend some time reflecting on three common ways to discern God's will: (1) Scripture study; (2) Christian conferencing; and (3) the direct intervention of the Holy Spirit. Were any of these used in the experience you recalled? How have you used these resources otherwise?

During the Day

One of the ways we pray "your will be done" (see Matthew 6:10) is as a declaration of obedience. Pray that as a breath prayer as you move through the day.

Group Sharing

Introduction

Two essential ingredients of a Christian fellowship are feedback and follow-up. Feedback is necessary to keep the group dynamic working positively for all participants. Follow-up is essential to express Christian concern and ministry.

The leader is primarily responsible for feedback in the group, but all persons should be encouraged to share their feelings about how the group is functioning. Listening is crucial. To listen to another, as much as any other action, is a means of affirming that person. When we listen to another, we are saying, "You are important. I value you."

It is also crucial to check out meaning. We often mishear. "Are you saying _____?" is a good check question. It takes only a couple of persons in a group, who listen and give feedback in this fashion, to set the mood for the group.

Follow-up is the function of everyone. If we listen to what others are saying, we will discover needs and concerns beneath the surface, situations that need prayer and attention. Make notes of these as the group shares. Follow up during the week with a telephone call or a written note of caring and encouragement. What distinguishes a Christian fellowship is caring in action.

Sharing Together

1. Begin your sharing together with a brief discussion of the theme of this week, growth in grace, and the necessity of discipline for growth. Ask the group: In what ways are

you growing? Are you practicing particular spiritual disciplines for growth? What are the disciplines that help you most?

2. Invite two or three persons to share their most difficult day with the study this week. Then invite two or three persons to share their most meaningful day.

3. In her teaching, Phoebe Palmer championed what she called "altar theology." In your reflecting and recording on Day Two this week, you were asked if there had been an occasion when you realized you must lay your life on the altar of Christ and become a living sacrifice, seeking to surrender your all to Christ. Invite persons who may have had that experience to share.

4. Spend ten to fifteen minutes (if time allows) discussing the meaning of complete or total surrender to Christ, otherwise known as "altar theology."

Praying Together

Hopefully, individuals are becoming more comfortable in this prayer time. Even so, be sensitive to the reservation of some to offer verbal prayer.

On Day Four, a portion of the hymn was offered as a prayer. Begin your prayer time singing that stanza of "Have Thine Own Way, Lord":

Have Thine own way, Lord! Have Thine own way!
Thou art the Potter, I am the clay.
Mold me and make me after Thy will,
While I am waiting, yielded and still.[20]

1. Spend two minutes in silence, reflecting on what was shared and praying for particular needs and situations that got your attention.

2. The leader should offer a closing prayer, or invite a volunteer to do so.

Donna
Ella + Aider

Week Four

The Means of Grace

What Are the Means of Grace?

They devoted themselves to the apostles' teaching and to fellowship, to the breaking of bread and to prayer. Everyone was filled with awe at the many wonders and signs performed by the apostles. All the believers were together and had everything in common. They sold property and possessions to give to anyone who had need. Every day they continued to meet together in the temple courts. They broke bread in their homes and ate together with glad and sincere hearts, praising God and enjoying the favor of all the people. And the Lord added to their number daily those who were being saved.

—Acts 2:42–47

"Means of grace" is a phrase used to describe the channels through which God's grace is conveyed to us. Wesley's interest in the means of grace spanned his life and pervades his writings. By this term Wesley meant "outward signs, words, or actions, ordained of God, and appointed for this end, to be the ordinary channels whereby he might convey to men, preventing, justifying, or sanctifying grace."[1]

In this workbook, we are concentrating on the necessity of spiritual discipline, with the emphasis on being disciplined in using the means of grace. Wesley never limited grace to these means, nor should we. God uses myriad ways of bestowing his grace upon us. Also, there are disciplines essential for our spiritual growth which would not be considered formal means of grace.

Wesley did, however, insist there are some specific ways God enables us to grow in grace. In his sermon "The Means of Grace," he also insisted that the means had no power within themselves. They were *means*, and using them did not guarantee growth; they open us to God's activity in our lives.[2]

Wesley discussed the means of grace in a number of different contexts with different emphasis, and differing lists from time to time. But most consistently, he divided them into two categories, and came out with this list:

Instituted means of grace, or works of piety: prayer, baptism, Scripture, the Lord's Supper, fasting, and Christian conferencing

Prudential means of grace, or works of mercy: Apart from attending upon all the ordinances, doing no harm and doing good.[3]

These means of grace are actually discipleship practices. Andrew Thompson, in *The Means of Grace*, stated:

Wesley saw the life of the early church as the perfect model for how the means of grace should be located at the very heart of Christian discipleship. A key Scripture passage comes from the Acts of the Apostles, which tells us what the first Christians did following their baptism: "They devoted themselves to the apostles' teaching and the fellowship, to the breaking of bread and the prayers" (Acts 2:42 [ESV]). From this fertile ground of practical faith, many fruits were borne. Acts tells us that "awe came upon every soul," that they met together daily and cared for one another's material needs, and that their hearts were made glad by the rich spiritual fellowship they shared (vv. 43–46 [ESV]). In fact, it was through their faithful use of these means of grace that God's gift of salvation was received. The passage concludes, "And the Lord added to their number day by day those who were being saved" (v. 47 [ESV]).

So it's no wonder that Wesley put great stock in the importance of practices like prayer, the Lord's Supper, searching the Scriptures, and robust fellowship. When he claimed that such things were ordained by God to serve as channels of grace into the lives of believers, he could point to a pretty solid biblical precedent! Since the time of the Pentecost, these are the very ways that God has been mediating his saving grace to the church.[4]

piety - quality of being religious or reverent

Reflecting and Recording

Spend a bit of time reflecting on the means of grace. Is this term familiar to you? Where and when did you first hear it? Which means do you presently practice? How faithfully? How have you experienced any of the means of grace conveying God's grace to you?

During the Day

Engage someone about the means of grace, simply sharing what they are, telling them about your journey through this study, and inquiring about their practices.

Disciplines and Means of Grace

The person with the Spirit makes judgments about all things, but such a person is not subject to merely human judgments, for "Who has known the mind of the Lord so as to instruct him?" But we have the mind of Christ.

—1 Cor. 2:15–16

As United Methodists, we have an equal and zealous emphasis on personal and social holiness. Wesley said it is "as tenacious of inward holiness as any Mystic, and of outward, as any Pharisee."⁵ Neither the mystic nor the Pharisee was a model championed by Wesley; at times he came near the edge of mysticism, and certainly a good part of his life reflected the model of a Pharisee who knew the law impeccably, and sought to diligently keep it.

To put the two together in this fashion, I believe, is one of those flashes of insight that comes out now and then in Wesley's writings. "As tenacious of inward holiness as any Mystic, and of outward, as any Pharisee"—that's a picture to hold in our minds as we think about the place of discipline in the Christian life, and of the means of grace as channels of growth and power.

In her usual disarmingly honest and challenging way, Mother Teresa painted the picture clearly in her confession: "Pray for me that I not loosen my grip on the hands of Jesus even under the guise of ministering to the poor."

Doesn't that say it? Isn't that our primary calling as Christians? Isn't that the way we will seek to live as the disciples Jesus calls us to be—gripping the hands of Jesus with such firmness that we can't help but follow his lead? As we have been insisting, following him in that fashion requires (discipline.) Also, as Wesley and the saints of the ages discovered: Christ and the church provide means of grace that assist us in the process.

Scripture, especially the New Testament, is replete with calls to a disciplined life. This is the process of sanctification. We may call it spiritual formation. Through spiritual discipline, opening ourselves to the shaping power of the indwelling Christ, we grow into the likeness of Christ. It was one of Wesley's primary concerns and a distinctive emphasis of the early Methodist movement that "the mind of Christ" grows in us. Deliberately chosen discipline is one of the marks of a Methodist style.

In the sermon Wesley preached in 1778 entitled "Some Account of the Late Work of God in North-America," he reflected on the fact that many of the converts of George Whitefield's preaching had fallen away because there was "no Christian connexion with each other, nor were [they] ever taught to watch over each other's souls."[6]

Wesley put a great emphasis on proclaiming the gospel, as did Whitefield. He never diminished preaching and teaching the Word, but he insisted upon the discipline of gathering with a class or a band. As the Methodist movement became more established, Wesley noted the deterioration of this discipline, and he warned against it:

Never omit meeting your Class or Band; never absent yourself from any public meeting. These are the very sinews of our Society; and whatever weakens, or tends to weaken, our regard for these, or our exactness in attending them, strikes at the very root of our community. . . . [T]he private weekly meetings for prayer, examination, and particular exhortation, has been the greatest means of keeping and confirming every blessing that was received by the word preached, and diffusing it to others . . . [W]ithout this religious connection and intercourse, the most ardent attempts, by mere preaching, have proved of no lasting use.[7]

Reflecting and Recording

Read Wesley's cautionary word again. How would it sound and what would be the response if your pastor exhorted the congregation of which you are a part in that fashion?

How would you characterize yourself and your friends in terms of how disciplined you are in spiritual practices?

How much teaching have your received related to spiritual formation? Do you give thought to the mind of Christ growing in you?

During the Day

Yesterday you were invited to talk with someone about the means of grace and this study. It is a spiritual-formation journey, with one goal being the mind of Christ growing in us. Be intentional about mentioning that today, and see what conversation ensues.

Transformed by the Renewing of Your Mind

Therefore, I urge you, brothers and sisters, in view of God's mercy, to offer your bodies as a living sacrifice, holy and pleasing to God—this is your true and proper worship. Do not conform to the pattern of this world, but be transformed by the renewing of your mind. Then you will be able to test and approve what God's will is—his good, pleasing and perfect will.

—Rom. 12:1–2

In our Methodist/Wesleyan tradition, we often hear, "John Wesley was a man of one book." We hear that often because it is true. He wanted Methodists to be Bible people. Early in the history of our movement, we were referred to derisively as "Bible Moths." Wesley's emphasis upon the primacy of Scripture was based on the conviction that through the Bible, God gives, confirms, and increases true wisdom. It is the Scripture which, according to Paul's word to Timothy, is "able to instruct you for salvation through faith in Christ Jesus" (2 Tim. 3:15 RSV). This instruction is for the full salvation that we are considering in this study. Scripture is essential for our "going on to salvation." Thus, Scripture is a primary means of grace.

But not just Scripture *talked* about, not the Bible laying there, or open on the pulpit. Wesley did not say the Bible was a means of grace. Rather, *searching the Scriptures is the means of grace.*

In today's scripture, Paul insisted to the Romans that we are transformed by the renewal of our minds. We are what we think, so study and searching the Scriptures is a necessary discipline for spiritual growth.

Most of the people I know must confess, shamefully, that study is not often high on their priority list as Christians. In fact, there is even a suspicion of learning in some churches and among many Christians. For some, to be smart and to be Christian are incongruent. A story from John Wesley's life (maybe a "Wesley legend") chides us here. He received a letter once from a pious brother who declared, "The Lord has directed me to write you that while you know Greek and Hebrew, he can do without your learning." Mr. Wesley replied: "Your letter received, and I may say in reply that your letter was superfluous as I already know that the Lord could do without my learning. I wish to say to you that while the Lord does not direct me to tell you, yet I feel impelled to tell you on my own responsibility, that the Lord does not need your ignorance either."

Knowledge of the truth is absolutely essential. Jesus affirmed it: "You will know the truth, and the truth will make you free" (John 8:32 RSV). To Jesus' word we add Paul's word to Timothy: "Study to shew thyself approved unto God, a workman that needeth not to be ashamed, rightly dividing the word of truth" (2 Tim. 2:15 KJV). Paul was specifically addressing Timothy in his vocation, urging him to distinguish himself from the false teachers by being a teacher of the truth. Yet his word has general application to us. The discipline of study is essential for "rightly dividing the word of truth."

William Barclay provided insight into this phrase by examining the Greek word for "rightly divide," which is *orthotomein*:

[It] literally means to cut rightly. It has many pictures in it. Calvin connected it with a father dividing out the food at a meal and cutting it up so that each member of the family received the right portion. . . . The Greeks themselves used the word in three different connections. They used it for driving a straight road across country, for ploughing a straight furrow across a field, and for the work of a mason in cutting and squaring a stone so that it fitted into its correct place in the structure of the building. So the man who rightly divides the word of truth, drives a straight road through the truth and refuses to be lured into pleasant but irrelevant by-paths; he ploughs a straight furrow across the field of truth; he takes each section of the truth and fills it into it correct position, as a mason does a stone, allowing no part to usurp an undue place and so to knock the whole structure out of balance.[8]

Reflecting and Recording

Repetition and memorization are principles of helpful study. Applying these principles, spend time memorizing Paul's word:

I appeal to you therefore, brothers and sisters, by the mercies of God, to present your bodies as a living sacrifice, holy and acceptable to God, which is your spiritual worship. Do not be conformed to this world, but be transformed by the renewing of your minds, so that you may discern what is the will of God—what is good and acceptable and perfect. (Rom. 12:1–2 NRSV)

During the Day

If you have not yet memorized these verses, copy them on a card. For the next four or five days, repeat this scripture often each day—when you awake in the morning, at lunch, and at random times.

Through God's Breathed Word

But as for you, continue in what you have learned and have become convinced of, because you know those from whom you learned it, and how from infancy you have known the Holy Scriptures, which are able to make you wise for salvation through faith in Christ Jesus. All Scripture is God-breathed and is useful for teaching, rebuking, correcting and training in righteousness, so that the servant of God may be thoroughly equipped for every good work.

—2 Tim. 3:14–17

Our *going on to salvation*, moving in sanctification, demands that we continue to grow. That admonition is expressed in a lot of different ways in the New Testament. In Colossians 2:6–7a, Paul said: "As you therefore have received Christ Jesus the Lord, continue to live your lives in him, rooted and built up in him and established in the faith" (NRSV). J. B. Phillips's translation renders it: "Just as you received Christ Jesus the Lord, so go on living in him—in simple faith. Grow out of him as a plant grows out of the soil it is planted in, becoming more and more sure of the faith."

George Gallup has been studying American opinions and attitudes for more than fifty-five years. Increasingly, he has been exploring the inner life of people. A few years ago, he cited six basic spiritual needs of Americans. Number five in that list was this: the need to know that one is growing in his or her faith.

The point is clear: After we have accepted Jesus Christ as Savior, we spend the rest of our lives bringing every aspect of our lives under the lordship of Jesus Christ. That's the process of sanctification and the purpose of the means of grace. That means we must choose to grow, to become stronger in our faith.

There's an old Chinese proverb that says, "Be not afraid of growing slowly; be afraid only of standing still." No matter the pace, if we are to continue to grow, Scripture is a primary means of grace and source for growth. Paul said Scripture is "God-breathed."

Does the designation "God-breathed" sound strange? Does the image challenge your senses enough to etch the truth solidly in your mind? When Paul says to Timothy, "All scripture is inspired by God" (2 Tim. 3:16 NRSV), he is literally saying, as per the New International Version translation, "All Scripture is God-breathed."

We don't have to get into a discussion about the words *literal* and *inerrant* as words to describe the Bible as God's Word. More important are the words *revelation, authority,* and *sufficient.* The Bible is God's revealed Word, providing revelation of God's self. The Bible is the authority of Christian teaching, and is sufficient in directing us to salvation, in being disciples of Jesus Christ, and providing the support, comfort, and strength we need for daily Christian living. That is what Paul is saying to Timothy in today's scriptural text: "All Scripture is inspired by God and is useful for teaching, for reproof, for correction, and for training in righteousness, so that everyone who belongs to God may be proficient, equipped for good work" (vv. 16–17 NRSV).

We could go on and on, talking about the Bible as God's breathed Word, or about the authority of Scripture, or about the harm that has come from our neglecting God's Word. For most of us, it is more important—and more needful—to focus on ourselves. That's where Jesus was leading his disciples in one of the last things he did while on earth: "Then he said to them, 'These are my words that I spoke to you, while I was still with you, that everything written about me in the law of Moses and the prophets and the psalms must be fulfilled.' Then he opened their minds to understand the scriptures" (Luke 14:44–45 RSV).

Opening "their minds to understand the scriptures" is a continuing ministry of Jesus. He does that through the Holy Spirit. Remember his promise? While he was still alive, he said to his disciples, "I still have many things to say to you, but you cannot bear them now. When the Spirit of truth comes, he will guide you into all truth" (John 16:12–13a NRSV).

There are two truths that relate to growth through the study of God's Word as the Holy Spirit illumines that Word for each of us. First, when our minds are open to understand the Scripture, our hearts are open to receive God's grace. Scripture puts it this way:

"Thy word is a lamp unto my feet, and a light unto my path" (Ps. 119:105 KJV). The Bible is the primary channel through which God's grace comes.

Then there is this second truth: When our hearts are open to receive God's grace, our wills are softened to do God's bidding. Get the movement: When our minds are open to understand the Scripture, our hearts are open to receive God's grace. And when our hearts are open to receive God's grace, our wills are softened to do God's bidding.

Certainly, it is easier to use Bible language than to obey Bible commands. Our wills being softened to do God's bidding has to do with whether our obedience is still law-centered or grace-centered. The growth that comes from studying God's Word, from immersing ourselves in Scripture, moves us more and more to graceful living out of grateful response for what God has done for us.

Reflecting and Recording

How does accepting the Bible as the God-breathed Word differ from your present under-standing? Would your use of the Bible change if you accepted it as God's breathed Word? How? Would you read it more? Would you share it differently with your friends?

Spend a few minutes reflecting on these two claims: When our minds are open to understand the Scripture, our hearts are open to receive God's grace. And when our hearts are open to receive God's grace, our wills are softened to do God's bidding.

During the Day

Engage someone today in conversation about the Bible by sharing Paul's declaration that the Bible is the God-breathed Word.

Persons of One Book

But as for you, continue in what you have learned and firmly believed, knowing from whom you learned it, and how from childhood you have known the sacred writings that are able to instruct you for salvation through faith in Christ Jesus. All scripture is inspired by God and is useful for teaching, for reproof, for correction, and for training in righteousness, so that everyone who belongs to God may be proficient, equipped for every good work.

—2 Tim. 3:14–17 NRSV

John Wesley claimed to be "a man of one book." In a moving personal testimony, he said:

I want to know one thing: the way to heaven, how to land safe on that happy shore. God himself has condescended to teach the way; for this very end he came from heaven. He hath written it down in a book. O give me that book! At any price, give me the book of God! I have it: here is knowledge enough for me. Let me be *homo unius libri* [a man of one book]. Here then I am, far from the busy ways of men. I sit down alone—only God is here. In his presence I open, I read his book for this end, to find the way to heaven.[9]

For the Christian, the Bible is the final authority for belief and action. We read other books and we discipline ourselves in study, but the Bible stands alone as the resource to show us how to live on earth as a Christ-follower and how to get to heaven. No discipline is more crucial for Christians than immersing ourselves in Scripture. No discipline provides more power and direction for spiritual growth than Scripture. For that reason, not only will we focus for a few days on this particular discipline, but all the spiritual disciplines we explore will be grounded in Scripture.

It is interesting that Wesley never says the Bible is a means of grace. As stated earlier, he says "searching the Scriptures is a means of grace." There is a difference, as Andrew Thompson reminded us:

> The difference has to do with how something can be a means of grace for us. Objects are not means of grace. They are just things. If we focus on the things themselves, we are likely to make idols out of them. Take the Bible, for example. You can walk around with it under your arm every day of your life, but it won't do you any good unless you actually read it. . . . For the word of God that is in Scripture to become a means of grace for us, we have to receive it actively. The means of grace are really about how certain objects and practices are taken up in an active manner in the spiritual life. We must engage them with our minds and hearts.[10]

Reread today's Scripture, underlining what you think are key words or phrases.

What did you underline? I can imagine that among other things you underlined *teaching*, *reproof*, *correction*, and *training in righteousness*. Let's look at these words and phrases as they call us to be persons "of one book."

Teaching. It is true that Christianity is not founded on a book, but on a living person. Before we had a New Testament, we had Christians and the Christian church. But not much time passed before it was necessary for these first Christians to present this living person, Jesus, by writing his story—the Gospels. So, now we get our firsthand account of Jesus and his teaching from the New Testament. The Bible is irreplaceable for teaching us who God, Jesus, and the Holy Spirit are, what they have done, and what they are calling us to be and do.

Reproof. We normally think of reproof as finding fault and criticizing, but here it means *conviction.* Scripture convicts us—confronts and convinces us—of our sin and error, but also of the pursuing grace of God, the forgiving love of Christ, and the empowering presence of the Holy Spirit.

Correction. Jesus assured us, "You will know the truth, and the truth will set you free" (John 8:32). The correcting work of Scripture is the testing of truth, and truth is wherever we find it. We must always use our minds, dedicating them to the pursuit of truth. The point here is that we are to test all theology, all ethical teaching, and moral codes by the Bible's teaching. The key to this testing lies in the teaching of Jesus as the Scriptures present them to us. That means that isolated teachings of the Bible must be tested by the revelation of God in Jesus Christ. In him, the divine yes has been spoken.

Training in righteousness. This is the end of it all—training in righteousness—and for what purpose? "That everyone who belongs to God may be proficient, equipped for every good work" (2 Tim. 3:17 NRSV).

Wesley's desire "to know one thing: the way to heaven" is the deep desire of all Christians. We were made by God for that purpose, finding our eternal rest in God. But we also study the Bible that we may live now a godly life, doing the will of God, being used by God for the salvation of others. We don't want to go to heaven by ourselves.

Reflecting and Recording

We have already practiced one way of immersing ourselves in Scripture: read a passage, underlining key words as a way to focus on meaning. Let's practice this again by underlining key words as we read this passage:

> Blessed are those whose ways are blameless,
>   who walk according to the law of the LORD.
> Blessed are those who keep his statutes
>   and seek him with all their heart—
> they do no wrong
>   but follow his ways.
> You have laid down precepts
>   that are to be fully obeyed.

Oh, that my ways were steadfast
    in obeying your decrees!
Then I would not be put to shame
    when I consider all your commands. (Ps. 119:1–6)

Using the key words and phrases you underlined, spend time reflecting on where you are in your Christian walk, and what changes you may be called to make.

During the Day

As you move through the day, stay aware of your time with Scripture. Is there any situation arising that might be impacted by recent scriptures you have studied?

More Than a Book

Now Moses was tending the flock of Jethro his father-in-law, the priest of Mid'ian, and he led the flock to the far side of the wilderness and came to Horeb, the mountain of God. There the angel of the LORD appeared to him in flames of fire from within a bush. Moses saw that though the bush was on fire it did not burn up. So Moses thought, "I will go over and see this strange sight—why the bush does not burn up."

When the LORD saw that he had gone over to look, God called to him from within the bush, "Moses! Moses!"

And Moses said, "Here I am."

—Ex. 3:1–4

Nothing exciting was going on with Moses. What he was doing was matter-of-fact daily work. Look at the first verse: "Now Moses was keeping the flock of his father-in-law, Jethro, the priest of Mid'ian; and he led his flock to the west side of the wilderness, and came to Horeb, the mountain of God" (RSV).

Nothing was out of the ordinary; he was just doing his work when God appeared. After years in Egypt, living in favor with the Pharaoh, there he was in Midian. His life had become routine—a keeper of the flock of his father-in-law—and then it happened. "And the angel of the LORD appeared to him in a flame of fire out of the midst of a bush" (v. 2a RSV). <u>The Bible</u>, more than a book, is not only the revelation of, <u>it is also an invitation and an encounter with, the living God.</u>

Moses experienced that encounter when confronted by the burning bush that was not consumed, and out of that bush heard the voice of God.

The encounter came to Elijah when, fleeing Jezebel, he was caught in the tumultuous upheavals of nature. But God was not in the shattering earthquake, or the torrents of rain, or the blistering winds. Elijah heard God in the still, small voice that thundered in his soul (see 1 Kings 19:9b–18).

Isaiah met God in the temple when, mourning the death of King Uzziah, he experienced God in worship, and God confronted him with this eternal call, "Whom shall I send? And who will go for us?" (Isa. 6:8).

John the Baptist, in his heart of hearts, had experienced the revelation. Flocks of people came out of the desert and Galilean hills to be baptized by John the Baptist in the Jordan, but no messianic notion overcame John as it too often does some leaders. He had encountered the eternal God who had an ultimate plan, so he could humbly say, "I baptize you with water for repentance. But after me comes one who is more powerful than I. . . . He will baptize you with the Holy Spirit and fire" (Matt. 3:11).

More than a book, the Bible is an encounter. And an invitation—an invitation to life!

The great events in the Old Testament: creation, covenant, and exodus, all reflect the gospel. The movement of God is a movement of love toward us. The big story of the Bible is the story of God staying with us—through his grace, wooing us, loving us, seeking to restore us to our created image, and bringing us back into fellowship. The last verse of the Twenty-Third Psalm says it so well: "Surely goodness and mercy shall follow me all the days of my life; and I shall dwell in the house of the LORD for ever" (v. 6 RSV).

If we miss that invitation in the Old Testament, we can't miss it in the New. It is an engraved personal invitation, personally delivered by Jesus Christ. He taught about it and preached it. He pictured it with pristine clarity for us in a series of parables in Luke 15: The Lost Sheep (vv. 1–7), The Lost Coin (vv. 8–10), and The Lost Son (vv. 11–32). One of the most beloved chapters in the Bible, this chapter has been called the "Gospel within the Gospel" because it contains the distilled essence of the good news.

If you miss the invitation in Jesus' teaching, you can't miss it in what he does. He writes the invitation in his own blood. He goes to the cross and bleeds to death for our sin, every drop of blood an expression of sacrificial love. Now that's difficult to comprehend, that Jesus would voluntarily, willingly, love us so much that he would die for us.

It's the ultimate in Jesus' life and teaching of a seeking, forgiving God who gives everything and goes to the limits to extend his invitation of life.

Reflecting and Recording

Spend some time reflecting on your Christian journey. How have you experienced the encounter and invitation of God through Jesus Christ?

During the Day

Engage someone today in conversation about God's encounter and invitation. Share your own experience, and invite them to share theirs.

A Blueprint for Living

How can a young person stay on the path of purity?
   By living according to your word.
I seek you with all my heart;
   do not let me stray from your commands.
   I have hidden your word in my heart
   that I might not sin against you.
Praise be to you, LORD;
   teach me your decrees.

—Ps. 119:9–12

The Bible is a revelation, an encounter, and an invitation; but more, the Bible is a blueprint for living.

Earlier we reflected on Paul's instruction to Timothy: "All scripture is inspired by God and profitable for teaching, for reproof, for correction, and for training in righteousness, that the man of God may be complete, equipped for every good work" (2 Tim. 3:16–17 RSV).

On Day Five, we reflected on a portion of Psalm 119. Today, we see in that same psalm a similar admonition to Paul's advice to Timothy: "How can a young person stay on the path of purity? By living according to your word" (v. 9). The Revised Standard Version is: "How can a young man keep his way pure? By guarding it according to thy word."

No greater resolve can come from any person than that. Then there is another word of the psalmist, "I have laid up thy word in my heart, that I might not sin against thee" (v. 11 RSV).

The Bible is a blueprint for living. When our minds are open to understand the Scripture, our hearts are open to receive not only God's grace, but also his guidance. Living with Scripture, the reality of God's grace prevails, and our wills are softened to do God's bidding.

Though we could pursue that in multiple ways, we concentrate on God's call to holiness, the overarching blueprint for our living "after God's own heart" (see 1 Samuel 13:14). Holiness is not an option for God's people. God makes it clear in his Word: "Be holy, because I am holy" (1 Peter 1:16). There ought to be something about us Christians that distinguishes us—in our ethical understanding; in our moral life; in the way we do business; in how we relate to others; and in the way we look at, and regard, the poor and the oppressed.

We considered holiness in Week Three as a part of our consideration of growth in grace. Richard Foster identified the holiness stream of Christian life and faith as one of the six traditions that uniquely identifies different denominational expressions of the faith. The holiness stream has been expressed in the Wesleyan/Methodist movements. The focus is "upon the inward reformation of the heart and the development of 'holy habits.' We can rely upon these deeply ingrained habits of virtue to make our lives function appropriately and to bring forth substantial character formation."[11]

One of the dynamic witnesses/teachers of the holiness stream was Phoebe Palmer. Her spiritual journey was long and painful, including the death of her daughter which resulted in the testimony we shared on Day Two of Week Three. Yet, long hours of prayerful searching and biblical study led her to what she would call her "day of days." This experience provided her the blueprint for living and led her to develop her "altar theology." She testified: "I received the assurance that God the Father, through the atoning Lamb, accepted the sacrifice; my heart was emptied of self, and cleansed of all idols, from all filthiness of the flesh and spirit, and I realized that I dwelt in God, and felt that had become the portion of my soul, my all in all."[12]

Holiness is at the heart of the Christian's blueprint for living. We must not forget that, though God's grace accepts us we are, it does not leave us as we are.

Reflecting and Recording

Spend time reflecting on the Bible in your life. If and how has it been a blueprint for living that brings us to wholeness and salvation, equipping us "for every good work."

Have you experienced the Bible as God's breathed word? How?

How might you be able to make it more a means of grace?

During the Day

Memorize this verse, and repeat it often during the day: "I have laid up thy word in my heart, that I might not sin against thee" (Ps. 119:11 RSV).

If you are a member of a group sharing this study, you will probably be meeting today. Reflect on your journey through the study this week. Is there any specific issue you want to talk about with the group?

WEEK FOUR
Group Sharing

Introduction

Paul advised the Philippians to "let your conversation be as it becometh the gospel" (Phil. 1:27 KJV). Most of us have yet to see the dynamic potential in a group that intentionally practices that kind of conversation. The King James Version of the word *conversation* is the word we would translate as "life"; thus, Paul's word to the Philippians.

Life is found in communion with God and also in conversation with others. Speaking and listening with this form of deep meaning that communicates life is not easy. This week focused on growth in grace and asked persons to share their most difficult and their most meaningful days. This may not be easy to talk about, but we want to work honestly at it throughout this study time together. Therefore, listening and responding to what we hear is very important.

To listen, then, is an act of love. When we listen in a way that makes a difference, we surrender ourselves to the other person, saying, "I will hear what you have to say and will receive you as I receive your words." When we speak in a way that makes a difference, we speak for the sake of others; thus, we are contributing to the growth-in-grace process.

1. Spend ten to fifteen minutes discussing the means of grace. Have you known about them? How important are they to you?
2. Look at the list of the means of grace on Day One. Which do you practice? Which does your church give attention to?

3. Invite two or three persons to share an experience of any of the means of grace having special meaning to them.

4. Discuss Paul's claim that we are transformed by the "renewing of [our] mind" (Rom. 12:2), and the role Scripture plays in that dynamic.

5. Spend ten to fifteen minutes discussing if and how Scripture as the "God-breathed" Word (see 2 Timothy 3:16) differs from your present understanding. Would your use of the Bible change if you accepted the Bible as God's breathed Word?

6. Read Wesley's confession about "one book" on Day Five. Discuss what it means to be a person "of one book."

7. Spend the balance of your time discussing the Bible as more than a book, focusing on the Bible as an invitation, encounter, revelation, and blueprint for living. Invite each person to share which of these descriptions they most identify with.

Praying Together

1. Praying corporately each week is a special ministry. Invite a couple of people to offer spoken prayers, focusing on what has been shared by the group in the sharing time.

2. Invite a volunteer to pray for the needs of your community's churches.

3. Since the Bible is a saving factor to anyone, invite a volunteer to pray that the Bible will be made available all over the world, but especially to someone in your community that has not yet been introduced to this "more than a book."

Week Five
Baptism and Holy Communion

Bonita - to be a believer

Madilyn - Wed 8:00 a.m. - cardiologist
10 yrs   passes out

Adrienne - cataract surgery - Tues

Frank

Dan - healing

An Outward and Visible Sign

We were therefore buried with him through baptism into death in order that, just as Christ was raised from the dead through the glory of the Father, we too may live a new life.

For if we have been united with him in a death like his, we will certainly also be united with him in a resurrection like his. For we know that our old self was cruci- fied with him so that the body ruled by sin might be done away with, that we should no longer be slaves to sin—because anyone who has died has been set free from sin.

—Rom. 6:4–7

Will Willimon is an outstanding preacher and a marvelous storyteller. Like many of us, he preaches what he writes, and writes what he preaches. I'm not sure if I read or heard his story of a young friend, age four, who was asked on the occasion of his fifth birthday what kind of party he wanted to have. "I want everybody to be a king and queen," Clayton said. So, he and his mother went to work, fashioning a score of silver crowns of cardboard and aluminum foil, purple robes of crepe paper, and royal scepters of sticks painted gold.

On the day of the party, as the guests arrived, they were each given a royal crown, a robe, and a scepter, and were thus dressed as a king or a queen. Everyone had a wonderful time. They ate ice cream and cake, then had a procession to the top of the block and back again. When it was all over, everyone knew it had been a royal, wonderful day.

That evening, as Clayton's mom tucked him into bed, she asked him what he wished for when he blew the candles out on his birthday cake. "I wished," he said, "that everyone—everyone in the whole wide world—could be a king and a queen. Not just on my birthday, but every day."

Willimon closed his story, saying, "Well, Clayton, baptism shows that something very much like that happened one day at a place called Calvary. We, who were nobodies, became somebodies. Those who were no people became God's people. The wretched of the earth became royalty."

In an unbroken tradition from New Testament days, the church has practiced baptism. With the exception of the Quakers, all churches fundamentally agree that baptism marks the entry into, or the identity of, a person with the body of Christ. In baptism, we are crowned as the people of God.

There are disagreements among Christians about the mode and meaning of baptism, but some things are held in common agreement. One, baptism is an outward and a visible sign of an inward and a spiritual grace. Two, the church employs the symbol of physical washing as a sign of moral and spiritual cleansing. Three, although the Scriptures give us few instructions, all agree that the sacrament of baptism is to be taken seriously. Baptism is symbolic of our passing from death to life through Jesus Christ. It is the sacrament of the church that marks the reclaiming of our identity, the fact that we have been named by God as his people through the church, that we nobodies have become somebodies. Peter expresses it graphically, "Once you were no people but now you are God's people; once you had not received mercy but now you have received mercy" (1 Peter 2:10 RSV).

In the earliest baptismal liturgies, after the person had been baptized, he or she appeared before the bishop. The bishop embraced the new Christian, then did something of great significance; the bishop dipped his finger into oil and made the sign of the cross on the Christian's forehead. This was known as the signation, "the signature." The sign of the cross upon a person's forehead was like a brand to show ownership. Just as sheep or cattle are marked to show ownership, so, too, Christians are marked by baptism to show Who owns them, and to what flock they belong.

Reflecting and Recording

Spend a few minutes pondering baptism. What are some questions you have? If you had to tell someone what baptism means, what would you say?

During the Day

Seek a friend who is a part of a different church than yours, and ask them how they practice baptism and what their understanding is of the meaning of baptism.

The Heavens Opened

When all the people were being baptized, Jesus was baptized too. And as he was praying, heaven was opened and the Holy Spirit descended on him in bodily form like a dove. And a voice came from heaven: "You are my Son, whom I love; with you I am well pleased."

—Luke 3:21–22

I'm amazed at the different perspectives that artists have of biblical events. My daughter, Kerry Peeples, was commissioned to paint a series for her church, giving witnesses to "the story." One of the events she chose was the baptism of Jesus.

If you see the painting, you will have to look intently before John the Baptist and Jesus being immersed into the waters of the Jordan come into perspective. If you are familiar with the scriptural record of his baptism, you will know why she portrayed the event the way she did. The descending Holy Spirit is dominant, bursting from the sky in powerful light and vibrant colors, so vivid you can feel the energy, and it takes no imagination to hear the booming voice: "You are my Son, whom I love; with you I am well pleased."

From his perspective, Jesus' baptism was a moment of personal decision and commitment. He had been doing manual labor in the carpenter's shop until he was thirty years of age. He knew that the time had come for him to leave his family, his friends, the carpenter shop, and the security he had grown up knowing in order to obey the call of God.

Certainly, Jesus was the Son of God. He was the Messiah. But he was also human, and as humans we make decisions and commitments which determine our destinies.

Jesus left the carpenter's shop and stepped into the muddy waters of the Jordan River. That was, first of all, a *decision*—a decision to follow God's destiny for his life. Again and again, Jesus said that he had come not to do his own will, but to do the will of his Father (see, for example, John 5:30; 6:38).

We have to keep reminding ourselves of who we are and what we're about. It was so with Jesus—even to the last. In the garden of Gethsemane, he was in so much anguish, so intense in his struggle, that drops of blood burst out as sweat to keep his whole being from exploding. "Let this cup pass, O God, if it is possible. But Father, as frightened as I am, as confused and frustrated as I am, as painful as I know it's going to be—not my will, yours be done!" (see Luke 22:42–44).

The process of deciding to be God's person, to do God's will, goes on every day and it never ends.

Not only was Jesus' baptism a decision, it was an act of *identification*.

John the Baptist was baptizing persons as a tangible sign of cleansing and commitment which came through confession and repentance. The questions arise: Why was Jesus baptized? Did he need to confess and repent?

John the Baptist had said of him: "One is coming after me who is greater than I . . . I am not even worthy to untie the thongs of his sandals." Then when he saw Jesus coming to him the next day, he said, "That's him—that's the one I've been telling you about—the Lamb of God who takes away the sins of the world. I baptize you with water to repentance; he will baptize you with the Holy Spirit and with fire" (see Mark 1:7–8; Luke 3:16).

And yet this "Lamb of God, who takes away the sin of the world" (John 1:29) seeks John's baptism. Who can probe the mystery of that?

This is certain: Jesus' personal commitment was not only to God, but also to us. In his baptism, Jesus stood beside us, making at that moment his identification with sinful human beings. His steps into the Jordan River were really the first steps that would eventually lead him to a skull-shaped hill and a crude, cruel cross. It was a costly identification. Still, Jesus was resolute; his baptism represented a personal identification with human beings.

In his baptism, Jesus acted out what had happened gloriously in his birth—the incarnation. God became one of us that we might become one with him. No other religion offers that—a God who identifies with us. Think what that means: you can't go any place where Jesus hasn't been, or won't go. There's nothing, Paul emphatically asserted, nothing that can "separate us from the love of God that is in Christ Jesus" (see Romans 8:38–39). In his baptism, Jesus become one with us.

Decision and identification are Jesus' baptism from his perspective.

Return to God's affirmation in today's scripture: "You are my Son, whom I love; with you I am well pleased."

Jesus had not preached a sermon. He had not performed a miracle. He had not called a disciple. Yet, he knew who he was. He had made his decision, had identified with the people, and now, he would never forget God's affirmation, "You are my Son."

When he was tempted in the wilderness, Jesus would remember this word of God. When he was anguishing there in Gethsemane, with the ominous shadow of the cross looming over him, Jesus would remember this word from God. And when he was hanging there on the cross, seemingly forsaken by everyone and all creation, he would remember this word of God spoken at his baptism.

Affirmation was God's response to Jesus and his baptism.

Following Pope John XXIII's Second Vatican Council, Douglas Steere, one of my spiritual mentors, called a small group together as The Ecumenical Institute of Spirituality. Though we met only for three days once a year, sharing our spiritual pilgrimages with one another, seeking to focus our minds and hearts on some growing edge, it was an important part of my life. Edward Farrell, a Roman Catholic priest who served an inner-city parish in Detroit, was a part of that group. I never will forget the insight he provided me regarding today's scriptural text and God's affirmation of Jesus. He said that Jesus went to the cross so that we, too, could hear the same word Jesus heard at his baptism, "This is my beloved daughter/son, with whom I am well pleased."

The voice which declared Jesus God's beloved Son is still speaking in our souls, "You are mine. You are unique and special. I am pleased with you. I love you. I love you so much that I gave my beloved Son for you. You are my beloved daughter/son."

Is it true with you, as with me? Without God's assurance, I'm left to compulsive seeking for security, pleasure, and meaning. Without an awareness of his grace, I exhaust myself at self-justification. I can't live with meaning and joy without the dove of the Spirit, God's invigorating, infusing, and inspiring power.

Reflecting and Recording

Reflect on the last few months of your life. What are some of the most painful, troublesome things that have happened? In the midst of those, would you have felt and acted differently, made different decisions, if you had remembered your baptism and heard God saying, "You are my beloved child, in you I am well pleased"?

During the Day

As you move through the day, listen for God's affirmation, "You are my beloved child, in you I am well pleased."

Naming and Claiming

After Jacob returned from Paddan Aram, God appeared to him again and blessed him. God said to him, "Your name is Jacob, but you will no longer be called Jacob; your name will be Israel." So he named him Israel.

—Gen. 35:9–10

Though it was written in 1976, many of us remember Alex Haley's novel *Roots*. That book and the TV miniseries produced from it was read and seen by millions of people on every continent of the world.

One of the most significant episodes captured in the television drama was recorded in the first chapter of the book: the customs concerning the birth, and especially the signal event of naming a child on the eighth day. That ancient naming ceremony of the African people involved the mother and the father taking the child out into the center of the village where the people assembled. The father took the baby from his wife's arms and, as all the people watched, he whispered the name three times into the ear of the child. It was the first time the name had ever been spoken, for the people felt that each human being should be the first ever to hear his or her own name. After whispering the name to the child, the father would announce it to the chief, and the chief would announce it to all the people.

In the television presentation, Kunta Kinte reenacted that great tradition with his only child. Against the wishes of his wife, who was afraid the slave master would discover they were still living by some of the customs of Africa and would punish them, Kunta Kinte took the risk. In the middle of the night, he took his baby, a girl, out into the night behind the barn, and reenacted that ancient ceremony of identity. He whispered her name three times in her ear and then lifted her face toward the heaven above his head, and in a marvelous, dramatic, moving moment, said, "Kizzy, behold the only thing greater than yourself!" It was a celebration of identity—a story to be told and an event to be kept alive in memory, in order to always know who we are.

It's a powerful image to recall as we give our attention to infant baptism. A great deal of confusion and misunderstanding surround this act of baptizing children, so we need to keep reminding ourselves of the primary meaning: an outward and visible sign of an inward and spiritual grace.

Baptism is not a new gift of Christ to the child, but the reaffirmation of Christ's perpetual gift to the church, of which the child is now becoming a member. Baptism is a proclamation to the church, and through the church to the world, that all persons live and move and have their being in God.

Children are already the recipients of God's grace; we baptize them because they are. Through baptism, a Christian learns who he or she is. It is the right of identity. When, in desperation, you may ask, "Who am I?" baptism would have you feel the water dripping from your head and say to you, "You are, in God's name, royalty. God's own, claimed and ordained for God's serious and joyous business."

Infant baptism becomes a great example of prevenient grace. If parents and the church fulfill their responsibility in relation to the child, baptism becomes a means of grace for that child, as they come to that point where they can claim for themselves the faith into which they have been baptized and nurtured.

What happens in infant baptism is not primarily an act of the parents, or of the child, but of the church, and even more so, of Christ in the church. We lose something of the real significance of baptism if we show more interest in the recipient than in the church that administers it and in the God who is acting in baptism. The sacrament of baptism is something which happens to the child and is done by the church on behalf of Christ. To enter into one's inheritance at baptism, to be named by the church on behalf of God as God's child, is not to receive an individual tincture of grace from the hand of the minister. It affirms that the child has a share in our common destiny—the common destiny of the church and the kingdom of God. So, in the laying on of hands with water, the minister acts on behalf of the church for the cause of Jesus Christ.

It is important to note that baptism is not only a means of grace for the one baptized; it is a means of grace for the whole church. Whether it is the baptism of an infant or the baptism of an adult, the entire congregation, in celebrating that baptism, goes back to the memory and meaning of their own baptism. We examine ourselves to see to what degree we have kept the faith, and how firmly we have clung to the cross which purchased our salvation. That means we should never be a spectator to baptism. We participate, taking up our baptism again, remembering who we are, named as God's people.

Reflecting and Recording

Spend a few minutes remembering your own baptism. If baptized as an infant, how did you learn of that baptism? How have you been nurtured in the faith?

If baptized as an adult, how were you brought to that point? Who played influential roles in bringing you to that point?

During the Day

Think of the persons who have played significant roles in your salvation journey, helping you in your life in Christ. Call or write at least one of them, expressing your gratitude.

Signs of Our Salvation

For in Christ all the fullness of the Deity lives in bodily form, and in Christ you have been brought to fullness. He is the head over every power and authority. In him you were also circumcised with a circumcision not performed by human hands. Your whole self ruled by the flesh was put off when you were circumcised by Christ, having been buried with him in baptism, in which you were also raised with him through your faith in the working of God, who raised him from the dead.

—Col. 2:9–12

Yesterday we considered infant baptism. We'll focus now on adult or *believer's* baptism, and the practice of confirmation which, in most churches, is the same. Central here is the self-conscious decision on the part of the individual being confirmed or being baptized to receive by faith the grace which God offers and which restores one into the family of God.

This necessitates a word about our entry into the Christian life. Consider this from the perspective of self-conscious persons. The goal toward which God is moving in our life through his prevenient grace is that each one of us will be personally and self-consciously aware of, and accept, God's grace in our own life. God's deep desire is that all would return from our sinful life in the far country, accept God's graceful forgiveness, and receive the new life he offers. This entry into the Christian life is called "conversion" or "new birth."

In our Methodist/Wesleyan and other evangelical traditions, there has always been an active stress on conversion and the new birth. Whatever our language, or our label for it, we hold that a decisive change in the human heart can and does occur under the promptings of God's grace, and that God, through the Holy Spirit, is working in each one of us to perform that grace. Such a change may be sudden or dramatic, or gradual and cumulative. Always, though, it's a new beginning; it is also a process. This means that our entry into the Christian life moves through a process. That does not mean there is a lockstep, one-two-three, as some would have you believe. It's not that at all. But there are movements to it, and ingredients which are essential.

There is awareness of sin; we are estranged from God and this brings feelings of guilt. Even these feelings of guilt are the work of grace in our life. God, in love, reminds us of his pain over our separation from him. Then comes repentance, the act of being truly sorry and turning around—turning from the old self to God. Repentance means being sorry for our state of separation, our waywardness, our estrangement, our independence of God, and turning to him for our salvation.

Next comes justification. By the grace of God, we're justified, made as though we were without sin. This happens through our faithful response to what God has done for us in the cross of Jesus Christ. Assurance follows. The indwelling Christ assures us of our salvation, giving us the confidence that John Wesley expressed when he said, God "had taken away my sins, even mine, and saved me from the law of sin and death." So, as stated in today's scripture, being "buried" with Christ is the language of baptism. More important, it is the fact of baptism.

I vividly remember seeing the Door of Death at St. Peter's Basilica in Rome. Pope John XXIII commissioned the eminent artist Giacomo Manzù to sculpt a new door for this great basilica, and the artist depicted on that door a series of death scenes. There was death by falling, death in war, the martyred death of Peter upside down on the cross, death by drowning, and others. I reasoned as I looked at that door, that this was behind the sculptor's theme: we enter the church by death. Baptism, our acted entrance into the church, is by water. So, death by water is a challenging and authentic understanding of baptism. The early church even built its baptismal fonts in the shape of tombs to make that meaning graphic.

Water is life, and also death. In baptism, both dynamics are present. We are buried with Christ in baptism, and also raised to newness of life.

Reflecting and Recording

Spend a few minutes thinking about baptism as representing death and life as a metaphor for your salvation journey.

During the Day

Often, when Martin Luther was depressed and undergoing strong attack from the devil, or sensed his courage and spiritual strength failing, he would lay his hands on his head and say aloud to himself, "I am baptized."

As you move through this day and the days ahead, whenever you are doubting your faith, or plagued with self-doubt, or oppressed by temptation, or aware of sin taking hold in your life, lay your hands on your head and say confidently, "I am baptized."

Proclaiming the Lord's Death

For I received from the Lord what I also passed on to you: The Lord Jesus, on the night he was betrayed, took bread, and when he had given thanks, he broke it and said, "This is my body, which is for you; do this in remembrance of me." In the same way, after supper he took the cup, saying, "This cup is the new covenant in my blood; do this, whenever you drink it, in remembrance of me." For whenever you eat this bread and drink this cup, you proclaim the Lord's death until he comes.

—1 Cor. 11:23–26

Along with baptism, the Lord's Supper is a sacrament. *Sacrament* is a word for something that is holy, so we call the Lord's Supper Holy Communion. As much as anything we do, this holy meal is a means of grace.

We need to look in the Old Testament to get the rich meaning of the Holy Communion which Jesus instituted at his last supper with his disciples. He was celebrating Passover with them.

Passover is one of the great Jewish festivals, and it commemorates their deliverance from the plagues God sent on Egypt when they were in captivity there. To avoid the final plague, the Hebrew households each sacrificed a lamb and spread its blood on their doorposts. While death came upon Egyptian households, the Hebrews and their firstborns were spared. Through the years since, Jews have celebrated God's deliverance with the Passover meal.

Jesus chose to spend his last intimate hours with his disciples by gathering them in an upper room for a Passover meal which Jesus turned into this sacrament for the church.

After the Passover supper, he took bread, blessed it, and gave it to his disciples saying, "This is my body given for you . . ." After they had received the bread, he took a cup of wine, saying, "This cup is the new covenant in my blood, which is poured out for you" (Luke 22:19–20).

It later became clear: the lamb Hebrew families had sacrificed in Egypt foreshadowed the sacrifice of Jesus on the cross, the Lamb identified in Revelation 7:17 who now sits on the throne in heaven. Through his teaching them at that Passover supper, Jesus prepared them for his own sacrifice, but also left it as a memorial for his followers to celebrate until he comes again.

Wesley called the Lord's Supper "the grand channel" of God's grace coming to us, and emphasized this in his preaching and teaching. The Lord's Supper was ordained by God to convey to persons according to either preventing, justifying, or sanctifying grace, according to their particular needs. The persons for whom it was ordained are all who also know and feel that they need the grace of God. No fitness is required but a sense of our state of sinfulness and helplessness.[1]

Wesley was convinced that this sacrament of the Lord's Supper was both a *confirming* and a *converting* experience of grace. He believed it should be celebrated as often as possible. Jesus commanded us to "do this in remembrance of me" (Luke 22:19b). Also, we do it often because of the possible impact and influence in our lives.

The dynamic of a confirming experience is in the vivid reminder of Jesus' love and sacrifice for us, and his ongoing presence in our lives. As we eat the bread and drink the wine, we remember that his body and blood were given for us, and we "proclaim the Lord's death until he comes" (1 Cor. 11:26).

Reflecting and Recording

Spend a few minutes reflecting on your experience of Holy Communion. Do you welcome or resist the experience? Why? Have you experienced it as a means of grace?

During the Day

Engage someone today to talk about the meaning of the Lord's Supper. Be honest in sharing your own feelings about this sacrament. Don't engage debate or argument; keep the conversation at feeling and thought level.

Christ's Presence in Holy Communion

As they approached the village to which they were going, Jesus continued on as if he were going farther. But they urged him strongly, "Stay with us, for it is nearly evening; the day is almost over." So he went in to stay with them.

When he was at the table with them, he took bread, gave thanks, broke it and began to give it to them. Then their eyes were opened and they recognized him, and he disappeared from their sight. They asked each other, "Were not our hearts burning within us while he talked with us on the road and opened the Scriptures to us?"

—Luke 24:28–32

I met one of my most interesting friends through the mail. With his letter, he sent a brief homily for possible inclusion in a series The Upper Room was printing. It was brief and didn't serve our purpose, but it was so powerful and so packed with meaning, that I wrote him immediately. That began a correspondence that continued for years. I soon learned that he was eighty-two years old, a Benedictine Monk, and living in a monastery in Lafayette, Oregon. That was the beginning of what has become for me one of the most meaningful relationships of my life.

I spent only one day meeting in person with him, but we exchanged letters often until his death. For most of the time on the day we spent together, we talked about the indwelling Christ and the presence of Christ in Holy Communion.

Four or five months after that day I spent with him, I shared in a national renewal conference sponsored by the Roman Catholic Church. The conference closed in worship, including the celebration of Holy Communion. Sadly, because of the Roman Catholic understanding, I wasn't allowed to partake of the bread and the wine. I wrote Brother Simon about this experience, and told him how painful it was.

By return mail, I received this letter:

My dear brother Maxie,

I made contact this week with the very soul of you, early in the week by mental telepathy and by letter. Wednesday and Thursday, my supra conscious started registering "Maxie, Maxie, Maxie," by its spiritual Morse dot-and-dash code, and that set me Hail Marying for the Dunnams. . . .

I asked Lady Guadeloupe [the patron saint of the monastery] *how to tell Maxie about Jesus in the blessed sacrament. She said "use Jerry* [my wife] *and the word* ontological." *So he, Jesus, is there ontologically, body and blood, soul and divinity, whether I think of him there or not. Why use Jerry? Kim* [that's our oldest daughter] *was with Jerry one month ontologically before either Jerry or you knew it. A living existence independent of your thought of it there, and how God willed her to be there.*

Do you get the picture? The fertilized egg growing in Jerry's womb that no one knew about until at least a month had passed. Brother Simon continued:

As a boy in church, I remember saying, "I wish I lived when Jesus did." The answer came immediately, "You are living with me. I am living with you." He's been living with me ever since. Sort of first-month, Kim like. I confess, occasionally, I tried to dodge his presence, but then my whole world crashed, and I hurried back, chastened and secure. Therefore, I can feel your pain in not communing completely.

He then told a story about children using their imagination:

I've been reading things about teaching children math. One teacher told her pupil, "Use your imagination. When I ask you, 'If you have 9 goodies in your right hand and 7 goodies in your left, how many have you?'" A pupil responded, "14." Teacher, "Wrong. 9 and 7 are 16." "I know that," the pupil answered, "but you said, 'Use your imagination,' so I ate 1 and gave 1 away. Therefore, 14 is the correct answer."

Is faith using your imagination in that fashion? And is this not the ecumenical key? In Holy Eucharist there are bread species substance, and Jesus substance. Your Maxie image in a mirror has no Maxie substance, but it's Maxie nonetheless.

As well as anything I know, Brother Simon's letter makes the point about the real presence of Christ in Holy Communion, which is relevant not just to the Lord's Supper, but to the whole of life. How beautiful his testimony! He heard Christ say, "You are living with me. I am living with you." And he responded, "He's been living with me ever since. Sort of first-month, Kim like."

This is Paul's concept of the indwelling Christ, coming alive experientially. Focus on Brother Simon's metaphor of my image in a mirror, having no Maxie substance, but being Maxie nonetheless. He was making the point about the real presence of Christ in the substance of bread and wine, but it goes even beyond that to underscore the daily reality of Christ's presence in our lives.

As today's scripture vividly affirms, at Passover the word became act at the table. The Lord's Supper is a resurrection meal, and we need not impatiently wait until some distant future when Christ will return from some distant past. The bread and the wine do not actually carry the flesh and blood of Jesus, but like our images in a mirror, they carry the reality of that presence. He is here, at the table with us.

Reflecting and Recording

Spend some time reflecting on Brother Simon's statement, "Your Maxie image in a mirror has no Maxie substance, but it is Maxie nonetheless."

How would you talk to someone about Christ being present at the Lord's Table?

During the Day

Seek someone with whom you can share about the Lord's Supper. Test Brother Simon's image with them: "Your Maxie image in a mirror has no Maxie substance, but it is Maxie nonetheless."

The Throne of Grace

Therefore, since we have a great high priest who has ascended into heaven, Jesus the Son of God, let us hold firmly to the faith we profess. For we do not have a high priest who is unable to empathize with our weaknesses, but we have one who has been tempted in every way, just as we are—yet he did not sin. Let us then approach God's throne of grace with confidence, so that we may receive mercy and find grace to help us in our time of need.

—Heb. 4:14–16

The appropriate invitation to every Lord's Supper should be, "Come forward to God's throne, where there is grace." We can approach every table of the Lord in confidence that, there, we can "receive mercy and find grace to help us in our time of need." As Wesley contended, the Lord's Supper offers both a *confirming* and *converting* experience of grace.

His claim is confirmed by focusing on one issue. Most of us are guilt-ridden because we do not accept the fact that, at God's throne, there is grace. It's a deep religious question—perhaps the deepest of all religious questions—having to do with the nature of God. Two stories illumine the issue.

One of them comes from South Africa. Alan Paton's novel, *Too Late the Phalarope,* is set in that land. A white police lieutenant has secretly carried on an affair with a black African woman. In South Africa, that was against the law in every way. Not only against the civil law, but in that stern, Dutch-Calvinist and racist society, it was an abominable, unforgivable sin.

The lieutenant is confronted with the charge by his captain. The lieutenant denies it, but the evidence is so overwhelming that he finally confesses. The captain does what might appear to be a strange thing: he goes to visit the lieutenant's father and tells him of his son's transgression. It's a moving and tragic scene.

The father asks the captain, "Is it true?"

The captain replies, "I fear it is true."

The father insists, "Are you sure?"

The captain says, "He confessed to me. It's true."

Then there is silence except for the sound of the father's deep breathing, like the breathing of some creature in agonizing pain.

In the room observing the scene is the father's wife (the son's mother) and also the father's sister. The father turns to his sister and says, "Bring me the book." She goes to the bookcase and pulls down the heavy family Bible and takes it to the man, wondering what passage he is going to read.

The fellow doesn't read any passage at all. Instead, he opens to the front of the book where the names of the Van Vlaanderen family have been recorded for 150 years in the Bible. He takes the pen and ink and crosses out the name of Peter Van Vlaanderen, not once, but many times as though to completely obliterate it from the page. Without any anger or despair, at least that anybody could see, and without any words, he abolishes the name. Then he turns to the captain and very calmly asks, "Is there anything more?"

The captain knows that this is his cue to leave the house, and he does, offering to the mother any kind of help he might be able to afford.

But the father turns abruptly to him and says, "No one in this house will ask for help." So, the captain leaves. Then the father, still sitting at the table, turns to his sister and says, "Lock the door, and bolt it, and bring me the key. The door of our house will never open again." That's the scene. The door is closed forever; the son can never return home.[2]

Consider another story; you know it. A father has two sons. One chooses to take his inheritance and leave home, spending it in riotous living. How differently this second story ends! When he comes to himself and decides to return home, the door is not closed, his name is not blotted out of the family; rather his father is waiting, welcoming, and ready to have a party of rejoicing (see Luke 15:11–32).

We can imagine how the son felt before he made the decision to return home. Nothing weighs more heavily upon us and drains more emotional energy than guilt. It's a painful reality in our lives. In fact, there are few, if any, human emotions that are as distressing and painful as guilt.

The Lord is waiting at his table, waiting not only to offer loving forgiveness and reconciliation, but confirming and sustaining power. When Wesley described the Lord's Supper as food, "strengthening and refreshing of our souls," he was talking about a means of grace for us now. Too many of us fail to respond to the invitation to come to the table, "so that we may receive mercy and find grace to help us in our time of need" (Heb. 4:16b).

Reflecting and Recording

Center for a moment on the father blotting the name out of the family Bible. Have you ever thought of God being anything like that? Do you know anyone who thinks of God in that fashion?

Did you think of the parable of the prodigal son before I began to tell his story? Is your story related to either of those stories? How?

Write a prayer, sharing with God how you feel after having considered those two stories.

During the Day

Share this verse with someone today: "Let us then approach God's throne of grace with confidence, so that we may receive mercy and find grace to help us in our time of need" (Heb. 4:16), and explain how it is connected with the Lord's Supper.

Emily - Germany
Deb - cancer
Ann - daughter car wreck w/ bike

Ann - sister concussion

WEEK FIVE
Group Sharing

Introduction

You are nearing the close of this study, with just this and two other planned group meetings. Your group may want to discuss its future, deciding whether or not the group may want to continue meeting together using another shared resource. Leader, test the group to see if they would like to discuss future possibilities. If so, and if you might want to continue as the leader, invite two or three persons to be prepared to make recommendations at the next group meeting.

In our Christian life and relationships there is often tension. This is certainly true in our sharing. As that is generally true in our Christian life, it is an issue in our sharing in small group community. We may have disagreement, and emotions are always involved when we are sharing deep convictions. Hopefully, you have cultivated enough trust in this group to share honestly.

In our sharing we always run the risk of being misunderstood, but our commitment to Christian conferencing should free us to take the risk. The way we listen and respond will free our fellow pilgrims to be willing to risk sharing. In your sharing, always take the time needed to ensure clarification. If you disagree with someone, check to determine whether you have heard rightly. Don't hesitate to ask questions. Even though you may feel deeply about what someone has said, and may disagree vehemently, you don't have to express that immediately.

Sharing Together

1. Discuss the meaning of baptism as "an outward and visible sign of an inward and spiritual grace."

2. There is common agreement among churches that baptism is:
   - a sign of moral and spiritual cleansing;
   - symbolic of passing from death to life; and
   - marks our identity as a Christian and member of the Christian community.

   What does each of these mean, and why are they important?

3. How many in the group have been baptized, and was it as an infant or as an adult?

4. Invite a couple of persons to share their experience of baptism. What led them to it and how did it happen?

5. Is there a person who was baptized as an infant who will share how they have been taught the meaning and what that means to them now?

6. Discuss Jesus' baptism as his identifying with us. Does it teach that in our baptism God is also saying to us, "You are my beloved . . ."?

7. Invite as many as will share to discuss what new insight on the meaning of baptism they received from this week's study. Don't ignore infant baptism.

8. Invite as many as will share to discuss what new insight on the meaning of Holy Communion they received from this week's study.

9. Discuss the real presence of Christ in Holy Communion. How was Brother Simon's observation, "Your Maxie image in a mirror has no Maxie substance, but it is Maxie nonetheless," helpful?

10. Invite a couple of persons to share their most meaningful experience of Holy Communion.

Praying Together

Many times, we are praying when we are not even aware of it. I have found this true especially in the hymns we sing. I have discovered that when I intentionally pray the hymn that is a prayer, it is far more meaningful.

1. The following is a prayer hymn. If the group knows it, sing it now. If not, read it aloud together.

> Break Thou the bread of life, dear Lord, to me,
> As Thou didst break the loaves beside the sea;
> Beyond the sacred page I seek Thee, Lord;
> My spirit pants for Thee, O living Word!
>
> Bless Thou the truth, dear Lord, to me, to me,
> As Thou didst bless the bread by Galilee;
> Then shall all bondage cease, all fetteres fall;
> Teach me to love Thy truth, for Thou art love.
>
> Thou art the bread of life, O Lord, to me,
> Thy holy Word the truth that saveth me;
> Give me to eat and live with Thee above;
> Teach me to love Thy truth, for Thou art love.
>
> Oh, send Thy Spirit, Lord, now unto me,
> That He may touch my eyes, and make me see;
> Show me the truth concealed within Thy Word,
> And in Thy Book revealed I see the Lord.[3]

2. Close your time together with the leader or a designated person praying a prayer of thanksgiving for how baptism and Holy Communion have blessed, and continue to bless, the group.

Week Six

Prayer

Prayer Is a Hunger and Thirst

As the deer pants for streams of water,
so my soul pants for you, my God.
My soul thirsts for God, for the living God.
When can I go and meet with God?

—Ps. 42:1–2

The prayer language of the psalmist is worth contemplating as we consider prayer as a means of grace. The psalmist poured out his soul to God; he cried, even screamed, from the depths of his being:

"My soul thirsts for thee; my flesh faints for thee" (Ps. 63:1 RSV).
"For God alone my soul waits in silence" (Ps. 62:5 RSV).
"O thou my help, hasten to my aid!" (Ps. 22:19 RSV).

He was confident that his soul's hunger could be satisfied only by the Lord. This confidence is dramatically demonstrated in the prayer language:

"My God in his steadfast love will meet me" (Ps. 59:10 RSV).
"I call upon God; and the LORD will save me" (Ps. 55:16 RSV).
"God is our refuge and strength, a very present help in trouble" (Ps. 46:1 RSV).
"For thou, O God, art my fortress, the God who shows me steadfast love"
    (Ps. 59:17b RSV).

Prayer is at the heart of the Christian life. If not *the* greatest, it is certainly at least one of the greatest privileges given us as Christians. It is a monumental means of grace.

You may or may not have had a meal yet today. But before the day is over, you will have eaten something—probably three meals, and maybe a snack between. Eating is natural and necessary. If you haven't eaten today, the chances are you have had a cup of coffee or tea, or a glass of water or milk. Drinking is natural and necessary. Like eating and drinking, prayer is not something foreign to our human nature. It is perhaps the deepest impulse of the human soul.

When Samuel Johnson was once asked what he considered the strongest argument for prayer, he replied, "There is no argument for prayer."[1] He did not mean that prayer is irrational or that there are not convincing arguments for the practice of it, but that prayer is so natural and universal, we need no argument for it. We all pray, and we pray because it is a part of who we are.

Prayer, however practiced, is an expression of our hunger for God. Augustine's word is more than a pious cliché: "Thou madest us for Thyself, and our heart is restless, until it repose in Thee."[2]

We will always be restless, always know the hunger and the thirst, because our resting in God is always of limited duration. We are sinners who too often prefer our way to God's way. Our pride does not allow us to be totally dependent on God. We move in and out of a trustful relationship with God. Even though we experience rest and meaning, purpose and joy, in times of yielding to God's will and way for our life, our bent to sin and self-reliance keeps pulling us away from that state of yieldedness and trustful relationship with God.

Prayer is a hunger and a thirst. The first beatitude of Jesus (see Matthew 5:3) in the Sermon on the Mount speaks to this issue. "Blessed are the poor in spirit" is the traditional translation of this text. "God blesses those who are poor and realize their need for him" is the way the New Living Translation renders it. Knowing our hunger and thirst for God is the condition for entering the kingdom—and for praying—the psalmist spoke the truth in unforgettable language: "As a deer longs for flowing streams, so my soul longs for you, O God. My soul thirsts for God, for the living God. When shall I come and behold the face of God?" (Ps. 42:1–2 NRSV).

Nothing other than relationship with God in prayer and worship can satisfy our hunger and thirst. It is a hunger to experience meaning, to know that life has purpose. It is a restless yearning to probe beneath the surface of our being, to penetrate the depth of ourselves and understand those feelings and notions and intuitions that come from we know not where. Prayer is something deep within us calling to something deeper yet, making us thirsty, restless, unsettled, even confused, because we are vaguely aware that we are not being and doing what we were meant to be and do. I like the way Edward Farrell expressed it:

> Prayer is like a journey, a journey which we can never cease making. It is like thinking, for each day a man thinks again, never knowing when he may turn a corner in his thought and find himself in a world he had never perceived before. Each day a man loves, but he never loves today exactly as he did yesterday, nor will he love tomorrow in the same way he loved today.[3]

John Wesley asserted that our Lord commands all who desire to receive any grace to pray:

> This is the express direction of our Lord. In his Sermon on the Mount Jesus puts it in the simplest terms: "Ask, and it shall be given you; seek, and ye shall find; knock, and it shall be opened unto you: for everyone who asketh receiveth; and he that seeketh findeth; and to him that knocketh, it shall be opened."[4]

Reflecting and Recording

Read Edward Farrell's description of prayer again and ponder it. Then, in the space beneath it, write it in your own words.

Prayer is like a journey, a journey which we can never cease making. It is like thinking, for each day a man thinks again, never knowing when he may turn a corner in his thought and find himself in a world he had never perceived before. Each day a man loves, but he never loves today exactly as he did yesterday, nor will he love tomorrow in the same way he loved today.

During the Day

Our praying is enhanced as we practice "breath prayer," a simple few words acknowledging God's presence and our desire to be present to God. Practice this breath prayer, voicing it aloud, or simply registering it in your awareness: "Lord, I thirst."

Prayer Is Fellowship with God

See what great love the Father has lavished on us, that we should be called children of God! And that is what we are! The reason the world does not know us is that it did not know him. Dear friends, now we are children of God, and what we will be has not yet been made known. But we know that when Christ appears, we shall be like him, for we shall see him as he is. All who have this hope in him purify themselves, just as he is pure.

—1 John 3:1–3

I indicated earlier that reading Scripture in different translations is a helpful discipline and means of grace. The first epistle of John, recorded in the translation I normally use, provides a marvelous description of who we are in relation to God. J. B. Phillips's modern English translation makes it even more lively:

Consider the incredible love that the Father has shown us in allowing us to be called "children of God"—and that is not just what we are called, but what we are. . . . Here and now we are God's children. We don't know what we shall become in the future. We only know that, if reality were to break through, we should reflect his likeness, for we should see him as he really is! (1 John 3:1a, 2b)

John had been with Jesus in the Upper Room. He had heard Jesus say,

Greater love has no man than this, that a man lay down his life for his friends. You are my friends if you do what I command you. No longer do I call you servants, for the servant does not know what his master is doing; but I have called you friends, for all that I have heard from my Father I have made known to you. (John 15:13–15 RSV)

In the context of this understanding of God like Jesus, who loves us and dies for us, and who wishes us to be his children who are his friends, we accept the simplest, most straightforward definition of prayer: *prayer is fellowship with God.*

We are persons in relationship. The uniqueness of being human is that we can enter into relationship with our environment, with other persons, and with God. The quality and depth of our personal relationships determine the richness of our lives. The highest and deepest and most meaningful relationship possible to us humans is fellowship with God. Our relationship to others and to our environment can never be completely satisfying, right, and whole, unless we have fellowship with God. The surest sign of fellowship, and that which builds relationship, is conversation—talking and listening to another.

Before we move on to discuss the dynamic of talking and listening as a way of praying, some more general observations about prayer are important. Prayer is not easy. As living beings, we breathe, eat, drink, and sleep. As human beings, we breathe, eat, drink, sleep, *and pray.* It's part of our nature as human beings to pray. This is one of the ways we express our natural hungering for God. Natural it is; easy it isn't!

There is a difference between the tendency to pray and the practice of prayer. We have the tendency to pray—the reflexive crying out in the face of pain or trouble; the spontaneous exclamation of joy in the presence of beauty, accomplishment, and fulfillment. We give expression to it sporadically according to the moods and circumstances of our life.

The practice of prayer is something else. To pray consistently is not easy; it requires commitment and discipline. Don't condemn yourself if you find praying difficult. Even those whom we call saints found praying difficult. Their journals and confessions reflect their struggles.

The disciples didn't find it easy. Remember the Gospel story: Jesus took his disciples with him to a place called Gethsemane, where he spent time in prayer as he anticipated the cross. "Sit here while I go over there and pray," he told some, then took Peter, James, and John and walked farther away. He was greatly distressed and troubled, and said to them, "I am deeply grieved, even to death; remain here, and stay awake with me." And going a little farther, he fell on the ground and prayed that, if it were possible, the hour might pass from him. After a time of anguishing prayer, he returned and found them sleeping—twice. When he came the third time, he said to them, "Are you still sleeping and taking your rest? See, the hour is at hand, and the Son of Man is betrayed into the hands of sinners. Get up, let us be going. See, my betrayer is at hand" (see Matthew 26:36-46 NRSV).

Prayer is natural, but not easy. Discipline is a part of the life of prayer. The purpose of discipline, however, is to enhance and increase the spontaneous dimension of praying.

Essential to using prayer as a means of grace is to stay aware of the fact that God is good, and we can communicate with God. This is an enormous assumption that needs to be fixed firmly in our minds. You, among all the millions of people in the world, can have personal communication with the Father.

The dominant image of God in the New Testament is as a Father. This was Jesus' descriptive word about God's nature. In the Sermon on the Mount, he used this figure to help us get our concerns into perspective:

> "Therefore I tell you, do not be anxious about your life, what you shall eat or what you shall drink, nor about your body, what you shall put on. Is not life more than food, and the body more than clothing? Look at the birds of the air: they neither sow nor reap nor gather into barns, and yet your heavenly Father feeds them. Are you not of more value than they?" (Matt. 6:25-26 RSV)

Reflecting and Recording

Reflect on each of the following claims about God in Luke 15. Does your praying acknowledge these images as reflecting God's nature and character?

God is like a shepherd who misses even one lost sheep from the flock (vv. 3–7).

God is like a housewife who sweeps a house clean to find one lost coin (vv. 8–10).

God is like a father who grieves for one prodigal son who has left home (vv. 11–32).

During the Day

Get the following scripture in your mind and memorize it:

Look at the birds of the air: they neither sow nor reap nor gather into barns, and yet your heavenly Father feeds them. Are you not of more value than they? (Matt. 6:26 RSV)

As you move through the day, be attentive to persons, especially children, and pray for and respond to them with this in mind.

We Pray to Experience God

O God, thou art my God, I seek thee,
  my soul thirsts for thee;
my flesh faints for thee,
  as in a dry and weary land where no water is.
So I have looked upon thee in the sanctuary,
  beholding thy power and glory.
Because thy steadfast love is better than life,
  my lips will praise thee.
So I will bless thee as long as I live;
  I will lift up my hands and call on thy name.

My soul is feasted as with marrow and fat,
  and my mouth praises thee with joyful lips,
when I think of thee upon my bed,
  and meditate on thee in the watches of the night;
for thou hast been my help,
  and in the shadow of thy wings I sing for joy.
My soul clings to thee;
  thy right hand upholds me.

—Ps. 63:1–8

To affirm that prayer is a hunger and a thirst—and that at the heart of it is mystery—is the place at which we begin our praying. Otherwise, we will be handling holy things with dirty and clumsy hands. However, we must go beyond this affirmation. For the Christian there is more. The God who made us for himself is like Jesus, who loves us to the point that he will even die for us. What a means of grace! To know that prayer is also a confidence, a confidence rooted in the belief that we are not alone in the world, that there is help beyond our human resources, that the hunger and thirst within us will be satisfied. It is the confidence that God made us for himself, and that our hearts will always be restless until we rest in him.

In that confidence, prayer becomes a privilege, not a duty. Many of us see prayer as a discipline, an obligation, something we *must* do. We've been taught that we *ought* to pray, and when we don't, we feel guilty. As a privilege, the discipline of praying becomes a creative freedom, not the bondage of duty. Consider this testimony of Sir Wilfred Grenfell:

> The privilege of prayer to me is one of my most cherished possessions, because faith and experience alike convince me that God Himself sees and answers, and His answers I never venture to criticise. It is only my part to ask. It is entirely His to give or withhold, as He knows best. If it were otherwise, I would not dare to pray at all. In the quiet of home, in the heat of life and strife, in the face of death, the privilege of speech with God is inestimable.
>
> I value it more because it calls for nothing that the wayfaring man, though a fool, cannot give—that is, the simplest expression to his simplest desire. When I can neither see, nor hear, nor speak, still I can pray so that God can hear. When I finally pass through the valley of the shadow of death, I expect to pass through it in conversation with Him.[5]

Read this testimony again, slowly and reflectively.
Now read today's scripture again.

The first sentence is a great personal claim: "God, thou art my God." As we asserted on Day Two of this week, prayer is fellowship. The heart of it is Communion—being with, in union, sharing.

Some say that they do not pray because God is not real to them, but a more accurate statement would be:

God is not real because they do not pray. . . . the practice of prayer is necessary to make God not merely an idea held in the mind but a Presence recognized in the life. In an exclamation that came from the heart of personal religion, the Psalmist cried, "O God, thou art *my* God" (Psalm 63:1). To stand afar off and say, "O God," is neither difficult nor searching . . . but it is an inward and searching matter to say, "O God, thou art *my* God." The first is theology, the second is religion; the first involves only opinion, the second involves vital experience; the first can be reached by thought, the second must be reached by prayer; the first leaves God afar off, the second alone makes him real. To be sure, all Christian service where we consciously ally ourselves with God's purpose, and all insight into history where we see God's providence at work, help to make God real to us; but there is an inward certainty of God that can come only from personal communion with God.[6]

Reflecting and Recording

Have you failed to pray consistently because God did not seem real to you? Do you see the implication of God does not seem "real because [you] do not pray"? Spend a few minutes pondering these questions.

During the Day

For prayer to be a means of grace, we must practice it. We practice it in many ways at many times. As you move through this day, pray this prayer often as an exclamation of joy: "God, thou art my God[!]" (Ps. 63:1).

Naming and Being Named

But now, this is what the LORD says—
he who created you, Jacob,
he who formed you, Israel:
"Do not fear, for I have redeemed you;
*   I have summoned you by name; you are mine.*
When you pass through the waters,
*   I will be with you;*
and when you pass through the rivers,
*   they will not sweep over you.*
When you walk through the fire,
*   you will not be burned;*
*   the flames will not set you ablaze.*
For I am the LORD your God,
*   the Holy One of Israel, your Savior;*
I give Egypt for your ransom,
*   Cush and Seba in your stead."*

—Isa. 43:1–3

Naming and being named is one of the most crucial needs of human beings.

I remember an experience with Mikail Gorbachev that brought this truth home in a fascinating way. Along with a twenty other ministers, we visited Russia at the time when the government was changing. As general secretary of the

Communist Party from 1985 to 1991, Gorbachev was the last leader before the dissolution of the Soviet Union.

Doctor Len Sweet organized our group. We daringly hoped for an audience with the general secretary; amazingly, it happened. We were given thirty minutes, but as our conversation progressed, he extended that time to an hour.

Because we were Christian and wanted him to know who we were and why we were in his country, we sought a way to communicate that in preparation for our meeting. We finally made the decision that we would do it in one of the questions we asked by saying to him, "Mr. President, as Christians we're persons of prayer. We know this is a time of upheaval in your country. Are there personal needs and concerns for which you would like for us to pray?"

We assigned that question to Dr. Sundo Kim. He was the pastor of the largest Methodist church in the world, located in Seoul, Korea, and the only non-American person in our group. It was providential that we assigned the question to him, because none of us Americans would have been as bold.

When we knew it was time for the interview to come to a close, we turned to Dr. Kim. Instead of asking the question, he said something like this: "Mr. President, we understand that you were baptized when you were a baby, and that your mother has been praying for you every day since." I'm not sure how he followed with the question then, but it was something to this effect: "Do you think that the grace of God is working in your life through her prayers?"

Gorbachev is a very charming man and has a wonderful sense of humor, but it was a tense moment. His face was red, and we could tell he became nervous; the question was burrowing deep. In order to relieve the tenseness, he used some humor. "Yes, I was baptized when I was a baby. When I was born my parents named me Victor. Isn't that a great name, Victor?" He became a bit relaxed, smiled, and continued, "But when I was baptized my grandfather changed my name. Maybe that's the reason for what has happened lately. I'm no longer Victor." Again, he paused, relaxed still more, and continued, "My grandfather named me Mikail; in English, that is Michael." And, totally in control now, he went on to say, "I've looked in the Old Testament, and I understand the name Michael in Hebrew means God's person." And with a sort of an impish smile, he said, "And that's not a bad name, is it?"

It was obvious, something deep had been triggered in his soul.

Naming and being named are the most crucial of all human needs. That is what God has been doing throughout history—naming and being named. That's the way it all began. As poetic as those first chapters of Genesis are, they express profound truth. God is about the business of naming. The natural order alone is not enough for God. So, persons for relationship are essential and are created, and God names them: male, female, Adam, Eve.

That creation and fall story reaches its climax when these new creations eat the forbidden fruit and suddenly become guilt-stricken; aware of their nakedness, they become filled with shame and hide.

Scripture says that God comes in the cool of the day, and calls them by name: "Adam, Eve, where are you?" And that's the way God seeks them. In Scripture, from that point on, some of the great movements have to do with God naming people, meeting them, calling them by name.

The coming of Jesus is the ultimate in God's naming activity. Again, the natural order alone was not enough; persons for relationship were essential. But that alone didn't do it, because these persons did not know in Whom they had that relationship. So, God appeared to Moses in the burning bush, and introduced himself out of that burning bush, saying, "I'm the God of Abraham, Isaac, and Jacob" (see Exodus 3:2–6). But again, that didn't do it. God had to become an Abraham, Isaac, or a Jacob. And he did—and his name is Jesus, the ultimate in God's naming activity!

But the dynamic goes on even beyond that. In one of those intimate moments with his disciples, Jesus was talking to them about the essence of things. In his Gospel, John records Jesus' using the beautiful metaphor of the vine and the branches to tell them who God was, who he was in relation to God, and who we are in relation to him: "I am the true vine, and my Father is the gardener. He cuts off every branch in me that bears no fruit, while every branch that does bear fruit he prunes so that it will be even more fruitful" (John 15:1–2, 5).

Jesus continues with a word of naming: "I no longer call you servants, because a servant does not know his master's business. Instead, I have called you friends, for everything that I learned from my Father I have made known to you" (v. 16).

It was in that context of naming us as his friends that Jesus gives us the most radical and extravagant word about prayer that you have in the Bible. "You did not choose me, but I chose you and appointed you so that you might go and bear fruit—fruit that will last—and so that whatever you ask in my name the Father will give you" (v. 17).

The most extravagant promise of prayer is made in the context of Christ naming us as his friends.

Reflecting and Recording

Spend some time thinking about how your praying might change if you took seriously that Jesus has named you "friend."

During the Day

Return in your mind to my story of Gorbachev. When he had talked about his change of name, Dr. Kim picked up the conversation, referring again to his Christian mother, saying something like, "We know how important your mother's prayers have been for you, and we want you to know, we are going to pray for you. In fact, I'm going ask Dr. Dunnam to pray for you now." The challenging admonition became reality: a preacher must always be ready to "preach, pray, and die." There will likely be a time today when it would be helpful and meaningful for you to simply offer to pray, or invite someone else to do so, and it would be a surprising means of grace.

Naming God and Naming Ourselves

My God, my God, why have you forsaken me?
Why are you so far from saving me,
so far from my cries of anguish?
My God, I cry out by day, but you do not answer,
by night, but I find no rest.

Yet you are enthroned as the Holy One;
you are the one Israel praises.
In you our ancestors put their trust;
they trusted and you delivered them.
To you they cried out and were saved;
in you they trusted and were not put to shame.

But I am a worm and not a man,
scorned by everyone, despised by the people.

—Ps. 22:1–6

Prayer is a relationship that moves from a third person, the remote "he" or "the Almighty," to the first and second persons singular, where we address God as "thou" or "you" in that intimate person-to-person sort of way. So, the first naming dynamic of prayer is *naming God as God is in our experience.*

There is no point in pretending when we come into the presence of God. That's the reason Martin Luther says that the primary requirement of prayer is to be honest. We simply name God as God is in our experience. And that experience is not always the same. In today's scripture, the psalmist prayed, "My God, my God, why have you forsaken me?" In another instance, he prayed, "The LORD is my rock . . . and . . . my salvation" (Ps. 18:2). One time he prayed, "I am like an owl in the desert, like a little owl in a far-off wilderness" (Ps. 102:6 NLT); at another time he prayed, "I sing for joy in the shadow of your wings" (Ps. 63:7 NLT).

Not only do we name God as God is in our experience, _we name ourselves as we are before God_. This is the confessional dimension of prayer.

The primary need for confession is simple: that we might experience forgiveness. The witness of the Scriptures is that the dominant desire in God's heart is the desire to forgive. David must have known this, so he prayed:

Have mercy on me, O God,
    according to your unfailing love;
according to your great compassion
    blot out my transgressions.
Wash away all my iniquity
    and cleanse me from my sin.

For I know my transgressions,
    and my sin is always before me.
Against you, you only, have I sinned
    and done what is evil in your sight;
so you are right in your verdict
    and justified when you judge. (Ps. 51:1–4)

Not only is it clear in the witness of David and the Old Testament, it is also clear in the New Testament that the dominant desire of God's heart is to forgive. The story of the woman caught in the act of adultery is a vivid witness. When the accusing men brought the woman to Jesus, it put Jesus in a no-win dilemma. If he elected to show mercy on the woman and free her, he clearly would have been disobeying Jewish law; if he condemned her or did not intervene in preventing condemnation, he would have been going against everything he had taught about compassion and forgiveness.

The accusers made their charge, but they were not prepared for Jesus' response. They must have been speechless, immobilized by Jesus' offer: "Let any one of you who is without sin be the first to throw a stone at her" (John 8:7). Jesus then bent over to write in the sand. Was he allowing the people some relief from their own engagement with him in order that they might deal with their own consciences? Or did he write something that probed even more deeply and burned more searingly upon their calloused hearts? Whatever the reason, when he arose, no one was present to condemn the woman, and Jesus announced to her his forgiveness and call to a new life.

For the adulteress and for the accusers, Jesus was offering an opportunity for confession and forgiveness. We could add witness after witness from Scripture. Beginning at the point of our believing that it is God's desire to forgive, confession becomes not a morbid discipline; not a dark groveling in the mud and mire of life; not a fearful response to a wrathful, angry God who is out to get us if we don't shape up. Rather, confession becomes an act of anticipation, a response to the unconditional call of God's love and the promise that "the blood of Jesus, his Son, purifies us from all sin" (1 John 1:7).

By confession, I don't simply mean the enumerating of our sins and failures, though that is a huge part of it. I mean honestly locating ourselves before God and sharing with God that which is at the heart of a vital interpersonal relationship. We can't have a meaningful relationship with another person unless we are willing to share with that person those things that are going on in our life: our fears, failures, joys, sorrows, pain, triumph, frustration, faith, or lack of faith. What is required of an intimate, meaningful human relationship is required in our relationship with God. We share with God in prayer all that is going on in our lives; we honestly locate ourselves before him.

This confessional dimension was practiced by Martin Luther King. One night in the middle of the tension of the Montgomery bus boycott, he was awakened by the phone.

An angry voice said, "Listen, nigger, we've taken all we want from you; before next week you'll be sorry you ever came to Montgomery." I hung up, but I couldn't sleep. It seemed that all of my fears had come down on me at once. I had reached the saturation point.

I got out of bed and began to walk the floor. . . . Finally I went to the kitchen and heated a pot of coffee. I was ready to give up. With my cup of coffee sitting untouched before me I tried to think of a way to move out of the picture without appearing a coward. . . . With my head in my hands, I bowed over the kitchen table and prayed aloud. The words I spoke that midnight are still vivid in my memory: "Lord, . . . I am here taking a stand for what I believe is right. . . . Now, I am afraid. . . . The people are looking to me for leadership, and if I stand before them without strength and courage, they too will falter. I am at the end of my powers. I have nothing left. I've come to the point where I can't face it alone."[7]

This is absolutely essential for our relationship with God to be real and lively. In our praying, we locate ourselves before God in terms of what is going on in our lives when we come to God. We name ourselves, and communion with God becomes real because of that kind of honesty.

Reflecting and Recording

What name do you give God in your day-to-day praying? Do you name God, as the psalmist did, in the way you are experiencing God in that particular time? Make some notes. How do you feel about God right now? Who is God to you, right now?

Allowing God to Name Us

That night Jacob got up and took his two wives, his two female servants and his eleven sons and crossed the ford of the Jabbok. After he had sent them across the stream, he sent over all his possessions. So Jacob was left alone, and a man wrestled with him till daybreak. When the man saw that he could not overpower him, he touched the socket of Jacob's hip so that his hip was wrenched as he wrestled with the man. Then the man said, "Let me go, for it is daybreak."

But Jacob replied, "I will not let you go unless you bless me."

The man asked him, "What is your name?"

"Jacob," he answered.

Then the man said, "Your name will no longer be Jacob, but Israel, because you have struggled with God and with humans and have overcome."

Jacob said, "Please tell me your name."

But he replied, "Why do you ask my name?" Then he blessed him there.

So Jacob called the place Peniel, saying, "It is because I saw God face to face, and yet my life was spared."

—Gen. 32:22–30

We continue our consideration of *naming and being named* as a dynamic of prayer. We not only name God as God is in our experience, and name ourselves as we are before God, *we allow God to name us*. We wait in the presence of the Lord so that he might name us. This is probably the most neglected aspect of prayer.

The most dramatic example of it in Scripture is the story of Jacob. All night long he wrestled with the Lord's emissary. We don't wait five minutes, much less an hour or all night. But Jacob stayed there, wrestling with the Lord. As day began to break, Jacob got a new name.

When I talk about God naming us, I don't mean that God is literally going to give us a new name. I mean that if we wait in the presence of the Lord, God will speak to us. Martin Marty said, "God comforts the afflicted and afflicts the comfortable."[8] That's exactly what he does. He speaks through our minds, giving us a new idea. He speaks through our emotions, stirring us up, or calming us down. He speaks through our imagination, giving us a vision of what might be if we get in tune with him and with his will.

God also speaks through our memory, and that's a tool always available for our use. Read the Psalms and note how often you come across the word *remember*. The psalmist said, "Why art thou cast down, O my soul? And why art thou disquieted within me?" (Ps. 43:5 KJV), and on and on he went, moaning and groaning, and then: "I will remember" (Ps. 77:11 KJV). That's the way God speaks to us. When our feeling relationship with God is not intact, when we may feel that we are walking through a valley of a shadow, when our lives are full of doubt, and we don't know the direction in which to go, and we certainly don't know the direction in which God would have us go, when there's no feeling the Lord's presence within us, we need to call on our memory and allow God to speak to us. Remember when he healed that loved one for whom we prayed, when he guided us around that perilous corner and saved us from destruction, when he restored a relationship and did away with an estrangement, and when he gave us the strength to go on in the midst of tremendous difficulty. Call on memory and, through memory, allow God to speak.

And surely, God speaks to us through his Word as we immerse ourselves in Scripture. He also speaks through persons. How many times has God's Word been brought to us through some friend who was sensitive to the Spirit and was used by God to speak the right word at the right time? In prayer we need to listen, and allow God to name us.

I didn't finish Martin Luther King's testimony which I shared yesterday. After having located himself honestly before God, saying, "I am at the end of my powers. I have nothing left. I've come to the point where I can't face it alone," something else happened. King said:

It seemed as though I could hear the quiet assurance of an inner voice saying, "Martin Luther, stand up for righteousness. Stand up for justice. Stand up for truth. And lo, I will be with you. Even until the end of the world."

. . . At that moment I experienced the presence of the Divine as I had never experienced Him before. Almost at once my fears began to go. My uncertainty disappeared. I was ready to face anything.[9]

That's prayer. We name God as God is in our experience, we name ourselves as we are before God, and we wait in the presence of the Lord to allow him to name us.

I'm not suggesting those are the steps you follow when you pray. I'm suggesting that this dynamic of naming and being named characterizes your prayerful relationship with the Lord. It will invest your prayer life with tremendous meaning, and make prayer the means of grace it is designed to be.

Reflecting and Recording

Spend some time reflecting on prayer as the dynamic of naming and being named. Examine the way you normally pray. Is the naming dynamic present?

One of the ways God speaks to us is through our memory. Recall an occasion when God was especially real to you. Rehearse that experience as you remember it; relive it as clearly as you can.

Do you think God may be speaking to you now, through that memory?

During the Day

On Day Three, I suggested that during the day you pray often as an exclamation of joy, "God, thou art my God[!]" (Ps. 63:1). Have you done so? Do it today. A repetitious practice such as this is using prayer as a means of grace.

Intercessory Prayer

Leaving that place, Jesus withdrew to the region of Tyre and Sidon. A Canaanite woman from that vicinity came to him, crying out, "Lord, Son of David, have mercy on me! My daughter is demon-possessed and suffering terribly."

Jesus did not answer a word. So his disciples came to him and urged him, "Send her away, for she keeps crying out after us."

He answered, "I was sent only to the lost sheep of Israel."

The woman came and knelt before him. "Lord, help me!" she said.

He replied, "It is not right to take the children's bread and toss it to the dogs."

"Yes it is, Lord," she said. "Even the dogs eat the crumbs that fall from their master's table."

Then Jesus said to her, "Woman, you have great faith! Your request is granted." And her daughter was healed at that moment.

—Matt. 15:21–28

Intercession and petition are such natural components of prayer, we must at least make note of their importance, especially as a means of grace. And you may wonder why we would turn to this scripture to do that. There are some attention-getting moments in this story. At first, Jesus refused to answer the woman's plea: "Jesus did not answer a word." How unlike Jesus! Can we learn about prayer from this?

Note that the woman was asking, as any of us would, for the healing of her daughter. She obviously believed and had faith, or she wouldn't have made this request. Need was there; faith was present; the prayer was worthy . . . yet no response from Jesus!

At this point the disciples begged Jesus to send her away. If the silence of Jesus to the woman's plea seems strange, what happened next was even stranger. Jesus said, "I was sent only to the lost sheep of Israel." You may have wondered whether Jesus was speaking to the disciples or to the woman, as what he said was so out of character with his ministry. It can't mean that the woman's request could not be responded to because she was a Canaanite and not of the house of Israel . . . Can it?

That response forever puzzles us, but what followed does not. The woman pressed her request: "Even the dogs eat the crumbs that fall from their master's table." She appealed to the love of Jesus. Acknowledging no right to a loaf, she asked for crumbs. When Jesus sensed this faith, in his love he responded, and the woman's daughter was healed.

Anthony Bloom has a marvelous comment on this story:

> So often we implore God, saying, "O God, if . . . if Thou wilt . . . if Thou canst . . . ," just like the father, who says to Christ: "Your disciples have not been able to cure my little boy. If you can do anything, do it" (Mark 9:22). Christ answers with another "if": if you believe, however little, everything is possible with faith. Then the man says: "I believe, help thou mine unbelief." The two "ifs" are correlative, because if there is no faith there is also no possibility for God to enter into the situation.
>
> . . . Whenever by faith the kingdom of God is re-created, there is a place for the laws of the kingdom to act, that is for God to come into the situation with his wisdom, his ability to do good within an evil situation, without, however, upsetting the whole world. Our "if" refers less to the power of God than to his love and concern; and God's reply "if you can believe in my love, everything is possible" means that no miracle can happen unless, even in an incipient way, the kingdom of God is present.

A miracle is not the breaking of the laws of the fallen world, it is the re-establishment of the laws of the kingdom of God; a miracle happens only if we believe that the law depends not on the power but on the love of God. Although we know that God is almighty, as long as we think that he does not care, no miracle is possible; to work it God would have to enforce his will, and that he does not do, because at the very core of his relationship to the world, even fallen, there is his absolute respect for human freedom and rights. The moment you say: "I believe, and that is why I turned to you," implied: "I believe that you will be willing, that there is love in you, that you are actually concerned about every single situation." The moment this grain of faith is there the right relationship is established and a miracle becomes possible.[10]

Here is a signal clue for our intercession: we begin by believing in the love of God as we see it in Jesus Christ, and we then willingly trust God to act powerfully in love. So, we can link our intercession with the practice of contemplative prayer as recognizing, cultivating awareness of, and giving expression to the indwelling Christ. We bring those for whom we are concerned into our awareness of the indwelling Christ; thus, we bring them to Christ. I doubt if there is a more powerful way of praying for another than to simply hold in our awareness a vision of the person for whom we are praying along with a vision of the loving Christ healing and tending to their needs.

Reflecting and Recording

Spend some time thinking about the matter of trusting, first, God's love, rather than God's power. Do you have difficulty trusting that love or believing in that power? Write some notes.

Spend some time now praying in this fashion for two or three persons about whom you are concerned. Get a vision of Jesus healing; think of the woman with the issue of blood touching the hem of his garment (see Mark 5:25–34), or the man living among the tombs (see Mark 5:1–13), or the blind man crying out from the crowd (see Mark 10:46–52). Now live in that awareness of the healing Christ, and bring those for whom you would pray to Christ in your own awareness.

During the Day

There are all sorts of signs around you to remind you of a cross. When you see such a sign, in your mind turn it into the cross of Christ. Let that remind you of the unstinting love of Christ and his care. When you think of a person or see a need, bring it into your awareness of the ever-loving Christ, and simply pray, "Heal, Lord Jesus."

WEEK SIX
Group Sharing

Introduction

Last week you considered the fact that you are nearing the close of this study. Since you have this and only one other planned group meeting, take a few minutes to consider where you are in your consideration.

Sharing Together

By this time, a significant amount of knowing each other exists in the group. People are feeling safe in the group, and perhaps more willing to share. Still, there is no place for pressure. With only this and one other group meeting, the leader, however, should be especially sensitive to one or two who may have been slow to share. Seek gently to coax them in participating. Every person is a gift to the group; the gift is fully revealed and received by sharing.

1. Spend fifteen to twenty minutes with persons sharing either their most meaningful or most difficult day with the study this week.
2. Discuss the meaning of prayer as a hunger or a thirst.
3. Invite a couple of persons to read their rendering of Edward Farrell's description of prayer as a journey, as recorded in Day One Reflecting and Recording.
4. Refer to the Reflecting and Recording on Day Two. Discuss your understanding of these images as descriptive of the nature of God.

5. Spend a few minutes discussing the claim that we pray to experience God as real. Is that a new thought? After the discussion, invite persons who will to share how that has been true in their lives.

6. Discuss how the dynamic of naming and being named is operative in your praying. Which aspects are present, which are missing?

7. Spend a few minutes discussing the prayer dimension of allowing God to name us, then invite any persons who will to share their experience of being named by God.

Praying Together

Let this prayer time be a time of intercession and petition.

1. Begin by being comfortably seated and quiet. Concentrate on the indwelling Christ abiding in you. Take a minute to cultivate your awareness.

2. Now, bring those for whom you are concerned into your awareness of the indwelling Christ; in doing so, bringing them to Christ. Rest for a minute or two in the confidence that the persons you have in your awareness are in the presence of Christ who abides in you. The loving Christ is healing and attending to their needs.

3. Move to a time of corporate petition and intercession. Invite the group to share persons and situations about which they are concerned, then two or three persons offer verbal prayers of intercession and petition.

Deb-discerning trial
Valerie Taylor-breast cancer (Marlene)
Cheri's friends — D+K travels —Heather

Week Seven

Acting Our Way into Christlikeness

With Fasting Join Fervent Prayer

"When you fast, do not look somber as the hypocrites do, for they disfigure their faces to show others they are fasting. Truly I tell you, they have received their reward in full. But when you fast, put oil on your head and wash your face, so that it will not be obvious to others that you are fasting, but only to your Father, who is unseen; and your Father, who sees what is done in secret, will reward you."

—Matt. 6:16–18

Fasting is perhaps the least practiced means of grace. Yet, both the Old and New Testaments teach fasting as a spiritual discipline. John Wesley saw it as a powerful means of grace and was concerned there was so much misunderstanding about it. Some people overvalue its worth, fasting to the point of doing damage to their health; others neglect it entirely, as if it has no importance at all. Wesley answered those misunderstanding in his sermon on fasting: "It is not all, nor yet is it nothing. It is not the end, but it is a precious means thereto; a means which God himself has ordained, and in which therefore, when it is duly used, he will surely give us his blessing."[1]

We deliberately consider fasting following our focus on prayer, because Scripture connects the two, and Wesley emphasized the connection: "And with fasting let us always join fervent prayer, pouring out our whole souls before God, confessing our sins with all their aggravations, humbling ourselves under his mighty hand, laying open before him all our wants, all our guiltiness and helplessness."[2]

Today, fasting is a lost practice. Though required of Roman Catholics in the past, since Vatican II, that is not the case. Most Protestants have no understanding of what fasting is, and few of those who do, do not take fasting seriously. Yet, fasting has always been a part of religious devotion, both Christian and non-Christian.

The Bible takes fasting for granted. Jesus assumed persons fasted. He didn't say, "If you fast," or, "You should fast"; he took for granted that people would fast. Twice he said, "When you fast." A large body of his teaching is in Matthew 6, which contains today's scripture. He used the same language to talk about prayer and giving to the needy as he did about fasting: "when you pray" (vv. 5–7) and "when you give to the needy" (vv. 2–3), seemingly putting fasting in the same category of praying and serving.

When the disciples could not perform a miracle, Jesus explained that it could be done only by prayer and fasting. Jesus fasted; the apostles fasted. Church leaders, including Wesley, and saints throughout the ages fasted. This being true, and the fact that there is the possibility of fasting being a means of grace, isn't it time that we gave it our attention?

We will continue our consideration of fasting tomorrow. For now, note there are wrong notions about fasting. We do not fast to prove how religious we are, or to be noticed by others. We fast to make more real our relationship with God. That being so, it follows that fasting is connected with prayer and, especially, repentance. It is false fasting when we make it an end in itself.

Reflecting and Recording

What kind of thoughts and questions go through your mind when you consider the fact that Jesus did not say, "If you fast," nor did he put effort into convincing you to fast when he said, "When you fast."

During the Day

Talk with a couple of people today about fasting. What is their experience compared to yours?

Perspective on Fasting

"Even now," declares the LORD,
"return to me with all your heart,
with fasting and weeping and mourning."

Rend your heart
and not your garments.
Return to the LORD *your God,*
for he is gracious and compassionate,
slow to anger and abounding in love,
and he relents from sending calamity.

—Joel 2:12–13

We closed our consideration of fasting yesterday by making the statement that there are wrong notions about fasting. We do not fast to prove how religious we are, or to be noticed by others. We fast to make more real our relationship to God. That being so, it follows that fasting is connected with prayer and, especially, repentance. It is false fasting when we make it an end in itself. God pointed out: "on the day of your fasting, you do as you please and exploit all your workers. Your fasting ends in quarreling and strife" (Isa. 58:3b–4a). God asked: "Is that what you call a fast, a day acceptable to the LORD?" (v. 5b).

In Scripture, fasting is most often connected with repentance. In today's scriptural text, the prophet Joel called the nation and people to repentance because the Day of the Lord is near.

Fasting is an outward sign of our genuine sorrow for sin. It is to be an external expression in denying ourselves, but also fasting and mourning is a matter of the heart. Until the heart is reached, every other act is just a meaningless formality and cold ritual. Our spiritual renewal must go far beyond just our outward activity, but at the very least it does begin there.

That is why the first day of Lent was called "Ash Wednesday." It was a special day of repentance. People went to church where they were marked with ashes while the priests intoned, "Earth to earth, ashes to ashes, and dust to dust," to remind the people that the wages of sin is death. Thus, people were called from their sin and urged to return to God. Fasting is identified with a change of mind and heart, a true sorrow for sin and the desire to do better. False fasting is when you go through the motions of fasting, but do not make any effort to change your sinful way of life.

Along with repentance, another dynamic of fasting is self-denial. When we fast, we learn to say no to ourselves. Without the ability to deny self, a person does anything he wants as long as he can get by with it. This is the reason we emphasize *practice* in considering discipline and the means of grace. We have to learn to say no to our self, and we need the power to say yes to difficult calls, so we practice self-denial.

Fasting is fruitful when it makes us choose top priorities in our life. To fast, we must decide who really is our God. What are the priorities in our life?

It is only as we fast that we learn the values and reap the fruit of fasting, yet it is important to name one other grace that comes. When we fast, in some small way we share in the sufferings of Christ. Granted, that fasting is small and trivial compared to Jesus' fasting, but it is better than nothing, isn't it?

Reflecting and Recording

Spend some time reflecting on where you are in relation to fasting. Do you fast? Have you ever fasted? Are you willing to give it a try?[3]

During the Day

Begin an experimental practice of fasting, maybe a meal a week, and connect your fast with an ongoing prayer week list you will keep.

Christian Conferencing

Brethren, if a man is overtaken in any trespass, you who are spiritual should restore him in a spirit of gentleness. Look to yourself, lest you too be tempted. Bear one another's burdens, and so fulfill the law of Christ. For if anyone thinks he is something, when he is nothing, he deceives himself. But let each one test his own work, and then his reason to boast will be in himself alone and not in his neighbor. For each man will have to bear his own load.

Let him who is taught the word share all good things with him who teaches.

—Gal. 6:1–6 RSV

In Truman Capote's *Other Voices, Other Rooms*, the hero is about to walk along a heavy but rotting beam over a brooding, murky creek. Starting over, stepping gingerly, "he felt he would never reach the other side: always he would be balanced here suspended between land, and in the dark, and alone. Then, feeling the board shake as Idabel started across, he remembered he had someone to be together with."[4] And he could go on.

Isn't this our experience? It has been mine. I shiver at the thought of having to go it alone. I get chills when I consider where I might be if, at the right time, I had not felt the board shake because someone was walking with me!

The Christian walk is a shared journey. We do not walk alone; others walk with us. John Wesley, deeply aware of this dynamic, made *fellowship* a dominant characteristic of the Methodist movement. The way he used the word vastly differs from the way we tend to use it. Andrew Thompson described the difference: "When we use *fellowship*, we use it as a common noun. It's simply what happens when people get together and spend time in one another's company . . . Wesley uses fellowship almost like a proper noun: Fellowship (instead of fellowship)."[5]

He had something specific in mind when he spoke of fellowship in the exploding Methodist movement of his day. The staid traditional congregations were being disrupted by the evangelism of this new movement, by their enthusiasm and public expression of zeal and passion. They wanted Methodists to be satisfied with the fellowship the normal routine provided through the parish churches in England. To their protestation that Methodist activities were destroying the fellowship they already enjoyed, Wesley argued they had no understanding of fellowship being fostered by this new movement. To those who claimed that Methodists were destroying the fellowship of the parish churches, Wesley responded bluntly:

> That which never existed, cannot be destroyed. . . . Which of those true Christians had any such fellowship with these [i.e., the false Christians who make up the majority of parish congregations]? Who watched over them in love? Who marked their growth in grace? Who advised and exhorted them from time to time? Who prayed with them and for them, as they had need? This, and this alone, is Christian fellowship.[6]

He used the word *conference* or *conferencing* for fellowship, and considered Christian conferencing one of the instituted means of grace. Wesley organized bands and class meetings to come together in small groups to focus on their faith, pray, share their experience of God, *confer* and seek advice and counsel, and confess their sins and ask for forgiveness. Paul described this conferencing (fellowship) in his letter to the Galatians, as best practiced in small groups who intentionally gather for genuine fellowship (Gal. 6:1–5). As noted, Wesley formalized this into bands and class meetings, and he charged Christians to "meet to minister grace to one another."

In today's scripture, Paul gave some guidance for our journey together. He called us to "bear one another's burdens, and so fulfill the law of Christ" (v. 2). He was talking about interrelatedness and interdependence. This principle is laced throughout Paul's epistles: "If one member suffers, we all suffer together; if one member is honored, all rejoice together" (1 Cor. 12:26 RSV); "We who are strong ought to bear the failings of the weak" (Rom. 15:1 RSV). The new life into which we have been born through Christ is a shared life.

Reflecting and Recording

Are you a part of a group that looks like what Paul was talking about? How much do you know about Wesley's bands or class meetings? Spend some time reflecting on whether and how you and the congregation of which you are a part are practicing this means of grace.

During the Day

Engage two or three persons you know from other congregations in conversation about Christian conferencing as a means of grace. Talk to them first about their understanding and experience of fellowship, then move to introduce the whole notion of fellowship practiced purposefully as a means of grace.

Listening in Love

They devoted themselves to the apostles' teaching and to fellowship, to the breaking of bread and to prayer. Everyone was filled with awe at the many wonders and signs performed by the apostles. All the believers were together and had everything in common. They sold property and possessions to give to anyone who had need. Every day they continued to meet together in the temple courts. They broke bread in their homes and ate together with glad and sincere hearts, praising God and enjoying the favor of all the people. And the Lord added to their number daily those who were being saved.

—Acts 2:42–47

This word of Luke describing the fellowship of the early church is an inspiring description of life together for Christians. The Greek word used to describe this shared life of the people of God is *koinonia*. Our best word for it in English is *fellowship*, but the English word is far too limited to encompass the meaning of it. Koinonia means all kinds of sharing: sharing in friendship (Acts 2:42), being partners in the gospel (Phil. 1:5), sharing material possessions (2 Cor. 8:3), having fellowship in Christ (1 Cor. 1:9), and sharing life together in the Spirit (2 Cor. 13:14). Above all, koinonia is fellowship with God: "that which we have seen and heard we proclaim also to you, so that you may have fellowship with us; and our fellowship is with the Father and with his Son Jesus Christ" (1 John 1:3 RSV). In koinonia, we are bound to each other, to Christ, and to God. Our life is a shared life. Because we belong to Christ, we belong to each other.

In every congregation I have served, I have emphasized the value of small groups, many times calling them Koinonia Groups. Wesley emphasized this dynamic as Christian conference and a means of grace. These groups, particularly bands and class meetings, were substructures of the Methodist societies designed to support members in responsible participation in the transforming work of God's grace.

These groups were in various forms; the most basic structure being the class meeting. Every person joining a Methodist society was assigned to a class of around a dozen members. The only requirement for joining was an awareness of one's spiritual need and a desire for God's help, so the range of spiritual need in the class was wide. A spiritually mature lay leader was designated for each class to help meet multiple needs. This leader visited every member weekly, inquiring of their spiritual growth, and providing comfort, guidance, encouragement, advice, and reproof as appropriate.

The band was different from the class meeting in that it was voluntary, and intended for those with some assurance of God's pardoning grace. The bands operated with mutual accountability rather than designated leaders.

A critical dynamic in mutual accountability is bearing and sharing burdens. Because we belong to Christ, we belong to each other. In koinonia, we are bound to each other, to Christ, and to God. Our life is a shared life; we hear one another's burdens.

As much as anything else, persons need to be listened to. As I asked before, Is there anything that enhances our feelings of worth more than being listened to? When you listen to me, you say to me, "I value you. You are important. I will hear and receive what you say."

When you really listen to a person, listening with ears and a heart that hears, it becomes revelation, and the Spirit comes alive in the relationship. Martin Buber, a great Jewish thinker, spent his life seeking to share with others the importance of relations between I and Thou. For the clue to this meaning, he referred to the role of Spirit: "Spirit is not in the *I*, but between *I* and *Thou*."[7] The Spirit is known in relationship; Buber would say *only* in relationship.

Perhaps not "only," but certainly relationship is the primary mode and place of revelation of Spirit. When I listen, the gap between me and the person to whom I listen is bridged.

A sensitivity comes that is not my own. I feel the pain, the frustrations, the anguish—sometimes feeling these and identifying a problem even when the other is not actually sharing the problem or these feelings. I listen in love and the miracle of "I-Thou" takes place; the sharing moves to the deep and intimate levels where the person and I really live. The Spirit opens doors and hearts and effects change. The miraculous thing is that I do not have to have an answer for the person with whom I am sharing. In my listening, I become the answer. If something specific is needed, the Spirit reveals the answer in the listening relationship.

Reflecting and Recording

We will continue this discussion tomorrow. For now, spend some time pondering your experience of fellowship. Have you experienced others genuinely bearing each other's burdens? What was the setting?

In what kind of setting have you experienced being really listened to?

During the Day

In your reflection, you probably called to mind persons who stand out as burden bearers, and a person who, at a critical time, made a difference in your life by genuinely listening to you. Offer a prayer of thanksgiving for them, and, if possible, contact them personally today to express your gratitude.

Available in Love

Brothers and sisters, if someone is caught in a sin, you who live by the Spirit should restore that person gently. But watch yourselves, or you also may be tempted. Carry each other's burdens, and in this way you will fulfill the law of Christ. If anyone thinks they are something when they are not, they deceive themselves. Each one should test their own actions. Then they can take pride in themselves alone, without comparing themselves to someone else, for each one should carry their own load.

—Gal. 6:1–5

A primary essential for participants in Christian conferencing is to be available in love. As of late, I have been asking myself how God is ultimately going to judge me and my ministry. I'm thinking it is here: whether or not I have been available in love; whether I have been Christ to others.

What does it mean to be available? We may best answer that by looking at its opposite. The unavailable person can't give themselves to others. They are too preoccupied with their own little world—their own functioning, their own reputation, even their own spiritual health. They are encumbered within themselves, and have well-defined dimensions to this private world. Others are judged, accepted, or related to on the basis of how they fit into this tight little circle. The unavailable man guards himself against involvement. We are afraid to love because we are afraid of what it may cost. We think our life is our possession. Since our time and energy are limited, we are protective of it by being unavailable.

What about the *available* person? He is not encumbered with his possessions. He doesn't set up too many categories, restrictions, or requirements for relationship. He isn't preoccupied with his own self-image. He is freed from the constraints of proving himself, so he has the capacity to listen and respond to the appeals made by others to him.

Jesus is our model for availability. It didn't matter that the crowd was pressing around him, he gave his attention to the woman with the hemorrhage who touched the hem of his garment (see Luke 8:43–48). It didn't matter that he had come to the cool shade tree at the well for rest; he entered into a totally personal relationship with that woman who came to the well at midday to escape the cold stares and vicious words of her fellow citizens (see John 4:1–42).

The marvelous aspect of this principle of availability is that we have to bring to a relationship only ourselves. It doesn't require particular skills and training. We simply have to be open and honest, willing to listen and share ourselves. Above all, we are to be available in love.

Too many of us fail in our fundamental calling to minister daily because we think we have little or nothing to offer or share. We need a heavy dose of self-understanding, self-appreciation, and self-affirmation, the integrity of the people of God. As Paul said in today's scripture: "For if anyone thinks himself to be something, when he is nothing, he deceives himself. But let each one test his own work, and then his reason to boast will be in himself alone and not in his neighbor" (vv. 3–4 RSV).

Unfortunately, the message that many of us have heard as the "Christian" message gives us little encouragement for self-appreciation. The message has come through as self-depreciation. To be sure, self-denial is at the heart of the gospel, but self-denial is not to be seen as self-depreciation, or any form of devaluating of the self.

Akin to misunderstanding this dimension of the gospel is a limited grasp of true humility. Christian humility is not a groveling "I'll-be-your-doormat" stance. We have thought of humility only as a recognition and affirmation of weakness and limitation. Not so. The truly humble know who they are; they know their strength as well as their weakness.

Paul did not stop by admonishing us not to deceive ourselves by thinking we are something which we are not. He went on to urge us to examine ourselves so that we will rejoice in ourselves. We need to learn to affirm strength. Christian character is not to be thought of in terms of weakness or anemic living. To be forgiven and accepted by God, to realize that he knows us thoroughly and loves us thoroughly, to be made a son/daughter and an heir is to be made a new person in Christ, to be given a vocation. Thus to be Christian is to be strong in God, for God, and with God.

Our strength, as Christians, comes from our relation to God and the people of God. We are directly related to God and, in the awareness of that relationship, we find our ability to move to action and to live for others, to be available in love.

Reflecting and Recording

Spend some time thinking about the understanding of life as a possession that the unavailable man hoards.

In the spaces below, write the names of two persons you have experienced as being available in love. In the space beside the names, make notes that describe their actions and relationship.

Contemplate an occasion when you were available in love to some person or relationship. What difference did it make in the person's life? In your own life?

During the Day

Make a prayerful commitment that, today, you are going to be available in love when the occasion arises.

To Be like Jesus

When the ten heard about this, they were indignant with the two brothers. Jesus called them together and said, "You know that the rulers of the Gentiles lord it over them, and their high officials exercise authority over them. Not so with you. Instead, whoever wants to become great among you must be your servant, and whoever wants to be first must be your slave—just as the Son of Man did not come to be served, but to serve, and to give his life as a ransom for many."

—Matt. 20:24–28

We have been dealing with what John Wesley termed, "instituted means of grace," which he called "works of piety": baptism, the Lord's Supper, Scripture, prayer, fasting, and Christian conferencing. We turn now to deal with the "prudential means," which he called "works of mercy." Apart from attending upon all the ordinances of God, Wesley listed two: doing no harm and doing good.

The lead theme of this study is Christian maturity, to be a saint. Simply and dogmatically, to be a saint is to be like Jesus. Accepting that assertion, we conclude, to *act as a Christian* is a means of grace. In our everyday life of acting as a Christian, which expresses itself in what we do and what we refuse to do, is a means of grace.

You may have noted that, as we considered Christian conferencing the last two days, this clearly underscored our acting our way into Christlikeness through listening and being available in love.

Clearly, there is a sense in which we act our way into Christlikeness. I've never seen a person who studied, or worshiped, or prayed their way into Christlikeness. But I've known countless persons who acted their way into Christlikeness. The likeness of Christ shines forth from their lives. All these persons pray; some of them are people with a deep prayer life. They study to varying degrees. They worship. But most of all, they are people whose acts of mercy make them look like Jesus.

Jesus, himself, in today's scripture, suggested what that looking like is: "whoever wants to become great among you must be your servant, and whoever wants to be first among you must be your slave" (vv. 26–27). *Servant* and *slave* are the big words here, and we don't like them. In a world which believes the strong man always wins, we don't like words like *servant*, because we superficially think servanthood means docile, submissive, capitulation to powers greater than we. But that is obviously not Jesus' understanding: "just as the Son of Man came not to be served, but to serve, and to give his life as a ransom for many" (v. 28). Being a servant was, for Jesus, the fulfillment of all he came to do. He accepted denial and mockery, scourging and crucifixion, in order that he might bear upon his own shoulders the weight of the sins of the world. He is the Suffering Servant portrayed in Isaiah 53: "upon him was the chastisement that made us whole, and with his stripes we are healed" (v. 5). Our Lord destroyed the power of sin by bearing "our sins in his own body on the tree" (1 Peter 2:24 KJV). That is servanthood. There is nothing docile or weak about it. It is the revelation of the strong grace of God; sin is forgiven at an unimaginably great price.

As Christians, we are called to be a servant of Christ, which means acting like him.

Reflecting and Recording

Spend some time reflecting on the following dynamics:

One, grace is bestowed to others through our acts of mercy. Make specific notes on some act of mercy you performed and how the receiving person was blessed.

Two, by our acts of mercy on behalf of others, grace is bestowed upon us. Think about the act of mercy you just reflected on. What happened in your life as you performed that act, or what happened as an aftermath of your action? What kind of blessing did you receive?

During the Day

Make sure that you perform at least one act of mercy today.

Servants after the Style of Jesus

It was just before the Passover Festival. Jesus knew that the hour had come for him to leave this world and go to the Father. Having loved his own who were in the world, he loved them to the end.

. . . Jesus knew that the Father had put all things under his power, and that he had come from God and was returning to God; so he got up from the meal, took off his outer clothing, and wrapped a towel around his waist. After that, he poured water into a basin and began to wash his disciples' feet, drying them with the towel that was wrapped around him.

—John 13:1, 3–5

The purpose of discipline is to work in such a consistent way, and with such a focus, that what we do for a time by deliberate and disciplined effort will eventually become spontaneous. That is the reason we must consistently use the means of grace.

The picture from the Upper Room where Jesus was eating the Passover meal with his disciples is the classic picture of Jesus as a servant. It is clear as we read the New Testament that serving was the most distinctive quality of Jesus' ministry. And Jesus left little doubt that this is the ministry style to which he calls us: "whoever wants to be great among you must be your servant . . . just as the Son of Man came not to be served, but to serve" (Matt. 20:26, 28). Not only does Jesus call us to this lifestyle, he gives life through it: "Whoever finds their life will lose it, and whoever loses their life for my sake will find it" (Matt. 10:39).

Not many of us want to be servants, do we? Also, there is a vast difference between the way most of us serve and Jesus' call to be a servant. The way most of us serve keeps us in control. We choose whom, when, where, and how we will serve. We stay in charge. Jesus is calling for something else. He is calling us to be servants. When we make this choice, we give up the right to be in charge. The amazing thing is that when we make this choice, we experience great freedom—true life in Christ. We become available and vulnerable, and we lose our fear of being stepped on, manipulated, or taken advantage of. Are not these our basic fears? We do not want to be in a position of weakness.[8]

Here is the conflict: even though we make the decision to serve, we continue to choose when, where, whom, and how we will serve. Thus, we continually run the risk of pride.

If we think we know others and their needs perfectly well, our serving will often hinder rather than help. To combat pride, we must be attentive to the other, intent on serving the genuine needs of the other, rather than serving our own need to serve. In this fashion, we will diminish the possibility of being on our own. We will be open to the Spirit to guide us in discerning need and in making appropriate responses to need.

Given a decision to serve, we must guard against two pitfalls. Our desire to serve may be poisoned by a desire to please. Also, there is the snare of turning our servant action into controlling power over another.

In the Bible witness, awareness of a calling to service is accompanied by a sense of personal unworthiness. This is the antidote to thinking that our salvation is connected with the works we do. In all our serving, we must keep alive the conviction that our salvation depends upon God's grace, not our performance. A part of that awareness is that our serving is not redemptive within itself. Our serving provides the environment, sets the stage, and releases the energy for the person we are serving to be genuinely helped, even healed.

The central issue is that we deliberately act as servants because we are servants of Christ. Thus, our choosing to serve elicits no false pride. In a disciplined way, we choose and decide to serve here or there, this person or that person, now or tomorrow, until we take the form of a servant, and our lives become spontaneous expressions of persons responding to Jesus' call: "If anyone would come after me, let him deny himself and take up his cross daily and follow me" (Luke 9:23 ESV).

Reflecting and Recording

Spend some time reflecting on where you are as a servant after the style of Jesus. Look at your acts of service over the past month, examining your service motive and style.

Were you serving a genuine need or serving your own need to serve?

Were you trying to please a group or a person you were serving?

Were you serving in any way to gain merit for yourself with God or with the persons served?

Pray for the gift of being critical in how you serve, yet for freedom to serve without being ponderous.

During the Day

Memorize this combination of two verses of Scripture: *"Whoever wants to be great among you must be your servant . . . just as the Son of Man came not to be served, but to serve"* (Matt. 20:26, 28).

Every day for the next three or four weeks, make this the text to keep in your daily awareness, repeating it to yourself at least three times daily at mealtimes.

If you are a member of a group using this workbook, today is your last meeting day. The group may have been discussing the possibility of continuing to meet. Pray for that discussion, read this week's Group Sharing guide, and be prepared to participate and make your commitment.

Group Sharing

Introduction

This is the final meeting designated for this group. You may have already talked about the possibility of continuing to meet. Before you begin sharing about your experience this week, complete those plans. Whatever you choose to do, it is usually helpful to determine the actual time frame so group members can make a clear commitment. Select some persons to follow through on whatever decisions are made.

Sharing Together

Note to leader: save about thirty minutes to respond to the last suggestion.

1. Begin your sharing by discussing fasting. What is your understanding of how and why we should fast? What is your experience? Why is fasting connected with repentance?
2. Invite anyone who is willing to share a meaningful experience of fasting.
3. One of the primary characteristics of Christian fellowship (koinonia) is Christian conferencing—mutual accountability and bearing one another's burdens. Discuss what that means and how it is to be practiced.
4. Discuss the principle of availability in love. How does that principle relate to listening in love and bearing one another's burdens? After a brief discussion, invite one or two persons to share a meaningful experience of being served by someone who listened and was available in love.

5. Invite one or two persons to share an experience in which they were the persons listening and being available in love, and the difference it made.

6. Take ten to fifteen minutes to discuss Jesus' style as a servant, how acting as a Christian is a means of grace, and how we act our way into Christlikeness.

7. Spend about thirty minutes for persons to share the meaning of this seven-week journey, questions they have, insights they have received, changes that have occurred, or commitments they have made.

Praying Together

1. Spend enough time to allow any person who wishes to pray a two- or three-sentence prayer, expressing gratitude for something particular that has happened to him/her as a result of this seven weeks, simply to express gratitude for the experience of sharing in such an intentional group.

2. Stand now for this final act of prayer and get into a circle, if possible, for the closing.

   A benediction is a blessing or a greeting shared with one another or by a group in parting. Take a person's hand, look into his or her eyes, and say, "The peace of God be with you," then the person responds, "And may God's peace be yours." Then that person turns to the next person and pronounces and receives the same blessing.

   Standing in the circle, let the leader begin to pass the peace to the person on his/her right. That person responds, and then turns to the right for the blessing to go to everyone.

3. Having completed the passing of the peace, speak to one another in a more spontaneous way. Move about to different persons, saying whatever you feel is appropriate for your parting blessing to that person, or simply embrace that person and say nothing. In your own unique way, bless each person who has shared this journey with you.

In koinonia we are bound to each other, to Christ, and to God. Our life is a shared life. Because we belong to Christ, we belong to each other.

Tommy - G's friend
Women - Cherie's friend
Heather - shoulder
14 yr old - anurysm
Cindy Gott - toe surgery

Donna - foot
Deb - trial
Marlene - cataract - Wed

NOTES

Introduction

1. James S. Stewart, *A Man in Christ* (London: Hodder and Stoughton Limited, 1947), 147.
2. John Wesley, "The Means of Grace."

Week One: Going on to Salvation

1. John Wesley, "The New Birth," in *John Wesley's Fifty-Three Sermons* (Nashville, TN: Abingdon Press, 1983), 567, emphasis mine.
2. Ibid., 573.
3. Karl Barth, *The Epistle to the Romans*, trans. Edwyn C. Hoskyns (Oxford: Oxford University Press, 1968).
4. John Wesley, "The Scripture Way of Salvation."
5. C. K. Barrett, *Black's New Testament Commentary: The Epistle to the Romans* (Ada, MI: Baker Publishing Group, 2011), 27, emphasis mine.
6. Kenneth J. Collins, *John Wesley: A Theological Journey* (Nashville, TN: Abingdon Press, 2003), 89.
7. William B. Fitzgerald, *The Roots of Methodism* (London: Charles H. Kelly, 1903).
8. John Wesley, "A Farther Appeal to Men of Reason and Religion" in *The Works of John Wesley*, ed. G. R. Craig (Nashville: Abingdon Press, 1989), 11:106.
9. John Wesley, *The Works of John Wesley: Sermons II, 34–70*, vol. 2, ed. Albert C. Outler (Nashville, TN: Abingdon Press, 1985), 97.
10. Albert C. Outler, *Theology in the Wesleyan Spirit* (Nashville, TN: Discipleship Resources, 1994), 58.
11. Wesley, *The Works of John Wesley*, 97.
12. Barrett, *Black's New Testament Commentary*, 27, emphasis mine.
13. Richard J. Foster, *Celebration of Discipline* (San Francisco: HarperSanFrancisco, 1985, 1988), 2.

Week Two: Walking in the Ways of God

1. Andrew C. Thompson, *The Means of Grace* (Franklin, TN: Seedbed Publishing, 2015), xviii.
2. John Wesley, *The Works of John Wesley*, vol. 3, bicentennial ed., ed. Albert C. Outler (Nashville: Abingdon Press, 1986), 59.
3. John Flavel, *The Whole Works of the Rev. Mr. John Flavel*, vol. 5 (London: W. Baynes & Son, 1820), 423, 428.

4. Richard J. Foster, *Celebration of Discipline* (San Francisco: HarperSanFrancisco, 1985, 1988), 2.

5. *The Imitation of Christ: Living Selections from the Great Devotional,* arranged and edited by Douglas V. Steere (Nashville: The Upper Room, 1950), 8.

6. Thomas à Kempis, *Imitation of Christ* (New York: D. Appleton & Co., 1844), 75.

7. Ibid., 13.

8. Ibid.

9. François Fénelon, *Christian Counsels: Selected from the Devotional Works of Fénelon, Archbishop of Cambrai,* trans. A. M. James (London: Longmans, Green & Co., 1872), 37–38.

10. *Selections from the Writings of Bernard of Clairvaux,* ed. Douglas V. Steere (Nashville, TN: The Upper Room, 1961), 21.

11. Richard J. Foster, *Streams of Living Water: Celebrating the Great Traditions of Christian Faith* (San Francisco: HarperSanFrancisco, 1998), 71.

12. *The Joy of the Saints: Spiritual Readings throughout the Year,* ed. Robert Llewelyn (Springfield, IL: Templegate Publishers, 1988), 108.

13. D. A. Carson, *For the Love of God: A Daily Companion for Discovering the Riches of God's Word,* vol. 2 (Wheaton, IL: Crossway Books, 1999), 23.

14. *Selections from the Writings of Bernard of Clairvaux,* 19–20.

15. Paul Thigpen, *A Year with the Saints: Daily Meditations with the Holy Ones of God* (Gastonia, NC: Saint Benedict Press, 2014), 84.

16. Jarrett Bell, "The Morning After," *USA Today* (December 7, 2000).

17. Ibid.

18. *The Joy of the Saints: Spiritual Readings throughout the Year,* ed. Robert Llewelyn (Springfield, IL: Templegate Publishers, 1988), 344.

19. C. S. Lewis, *Mere Christianity* (New York: Macmillan Publishing Company, 1952), 158.

20. Edwin Hatch, "Breathe on Me, Breath of God," 1878, public domain.

Week Three: Growth in Grace

1. Paul Thigpen, *A Year with the Saints: Daily Meditations with the Holy Ones of God* (Gastonia, NC: Saint Benedict Press, 2014), 2.

2. M. Scott Peck, *The Road Less Traveled: A New Psychology of Love, Traditional Values, and Spiritual Growth* (New York: Simon & Schuster, 1978), 77.

3. Richard J. Foster, *Streams of Living Water: Celebrating the Great Traditions of Christian Faith* (San Francisco: HarperSanFrancisco, 1998), 61.

4. Charles Edward White, "Phoebe Palmer and the Development of Pentecostal Pneumatology," *Wesleyan Theological Journal* (Spring–Fall 1988): 208.

5. Phoebe Palmer, *Phoebe Palmer: Selected Writings,* ed. Thomas C. Oden (Mahwah, NJ: Paulist Press, 1988), 99–100.

6. Foster, *Streams of Living Water*, 65.
7. Thomas à Kempis, *Imitation of Christ* (New York: D. Appleton & Co., 1844), 144–45.
8. Judson W. Van DeVenter, "I Surrender All," 1896, public domain.
9. *The Joy of the Saints: Spiritual Readings throughout the Year*, ed. Robert Llewelyn (Springfield, IL: Templegate Publishers, 1988), 69.
10. Foster, *Streams of Living Water*, 133.
11. Kathleen Norris, *The Cloister Walk* (New York: Riverhead Books, 1997), xvii.
12. Ibid., xvii–xviii.
13. Ibid., xviii.
14. John Wesley, *The Works of the Rev. John Wesley*, vol. 10 (New York: J. & J. Harper, 1827), 415–16.
15. Adelaide A. Pollard, "Have Thine Own Way, Lord," 1907, public domain.
16. Ibid.
17. Simone Weil, *Waiting on God* (London: Collins Fontana, 1963), 75.
18. Ibid.
19. Thigpen, *A Year with the Saints*, 249.
20. Pollard, "Have Thine Own Way, Lord."

Week Four: The Means of Grace

1. John Wesley, "The Means of Grace" Sermon 16.
2. John Wesley, *Wesley's Fifty-Three Sermons*, "The Means of Grace"; ed. Edward H. Sugden in *The Works of Wesley*, 18 vols. (Grand Rapids: Zondervan, 1986).
3. Ibid.
4. Andrew C. Thompson, *The Means of Grace: Traditioned Practice in Today's World* (Franklin, TN: Seedbed Publishing, 2015), 16–17.
5. John Wesley, "On God's Vineyard"; http://www.godrules.net/library/wsermons/wsermons107.htm.
6. John Wesley, "Some Account of the Late Work of God in North-America," 411.
7. John Wesley, "A Plain Account of Christian Perfection," in *The Works of John Wesley*, 14 vols., ed. Thomas Jackson (Grand Rapids: Baker Book House, 1978), 11:433.
8. William Barclay, "The Letters to Timothy, Titus and Philemon" in *The New Daily Study Bible* (Louisville, KY: Westminster John Knox Press, 1975), 198–99.
9. John Wesley, *Wesley's Fifty-Three Sermons*, ed. Edward H. Sugden (Nashville, TN: Abingdon, 1983). This quotation is taken from the preface to his sermons.
10. Thompson, *The Means of Grace*, 39.
11. Richard J. Foster, *Streams of Living Water: Celebrating the Great Traditions of Christian Faith* (San Francisco: HarperSanFrancisco, 1998), 61.
12. Phoebe Palmer, *Phoebe Palmer: Selected Writings*, 115, quoted by Foster in *Streams of Living Water*, 65.

Week Five: Baptism and Holy Communion

1. *The Works of John Wesley,* 14 vols., ed. Thomas Jackson (Grand Rapids: Zondervan, 1958).
2. Alan Paton, *Too Late the Phalarope* (New York: Scribner, 1996).
3. Mary Artemisia Lathbury, "Break Thou the Bread of Life," 1877, public domain.

Week Six: Prayer

1. G. W. Hockley, "Prayer and Communion," in *Report of the First Anglo-Catholic Congress: London, 1920* (New York: The Macmillan Company, 1920), 162.
2. Augustine, *The Confessions of Saint Augustine,* trans. Edward B. Pusey (Grand Rapids, MI: Christian Classics Ethereal Library; Oak Harbor, WA: Logos Research Systems, Inc., 1999), 17, public domain.
3. Edward J. Farrell, *Prayer Is a Hunger* (Denville, NJ: Dimension Books, 1972), 11.
4. John Wesley, *The Works of John Wesley: Sermons I,* ed. Albert C. Outler (Nashville, TN: Abingdon Press, 1985), 255–58.
5. Wilfred T. Grenfell, "Dr. Wilfred T. Grenfell on Prayer," in "The Sanctuary," *The Christian Advocate* (New York: Nov. 6, 1913), vol. 88, 17.
6. Harry Emerson Fosdick, *The Meaning of Prayer* (New York: Association Press, 1916), 36.
7. Martin Luther King, Jr., *The Autobiography of Martin Luther King, Jr.,* ed. Clayborne Carson (New York: IPM/Warner Books, 2001).
8. Martin E. Marty, *Religion and Republic: The American Circumstance* (Boston: Beacon Press, 1987). Marty adapted the phrase that was originally coined in reference to "the newspaper" by Finley Peter Dunne through his fictional *Chicago Evening Post* character, Mr. Dooley, in 1902.
9. King, *The Autobiography of Martin Luther King Jr.*
10. Anthony Bloom, *Living Prayer* (London: Darton, Longman and Todd, 1966), 70–72.

Week Seven: Acting Our Way into Christlikeness

1. Jackson, op. cit. John Wesley, "Upon Our Lord's Sermon on the Mount VII," IV.46, in *Works of John Wesley 1:610–11.*
2. Ibid.
3. Andrew Thompson's book, *The Means of Grace: Traditioned Practice in Today's World* (Franklin, TN: Seedbed Publishing, 2015) has a chapter on fasting. The book also includes discussion of the means of grace we have considered in this workbook, as well as a helpful discussion of classes and bands, which were a core dynamic of John Wesley's call to holy living. You may want to get that book, or find other resources for further consideration of fasting. World Methodist Evangelism has a program, "The Wesleyan Pattern of Prayer and Fasting," to which we are

invited. In more than 130 countries, the Wesleyan family joins in the same weekly fashion, which John Wesley observed most of his life: going without solid food after their evening meal each Thursday until mid-afternoon each Friday. This time of fasting is focused in prayer on the vision that those who follow Jesus would be empowered to become channels for the transforming power of the Holy Spirit. You may pursue your interest at info@worldmethodist.org.

4. Truman Capote, *Other Voices, Other Rooms* (New York: Vintage Books, 2012), 144.
5. Thompson, *The Means of Grace*, 87–88.
6. John Wesley, "A Plain Account of the People Called Methodists"; http://www.godrules.net/library/wesley/274wesley_h6.htm.
7. Martin Buber, *I and Thou*, trans. Ronald Gregor Smith (Edinburgh: T. & T. Clark, 1937), 39; http://www.maximusveritas.com/wp-content/uploads/2016/04/iandthou.pdf.
8. Maxie Dunnam, *Alive in Christ: The Dynamic Process of Spiritual Formation* (Nashville, TN: Abingdon Press, 1987), 150.

CPSIA information can be obtained
at www.ICGtesting.com
Printed in the USA
LVHW060403250721
693454LV00001B/1